"Fire provides light and warmth, or it can bring pain and destruction. Addie tells us a story in which her fiery faith sparked both outcomes and how she's worked to contain those flames. She walks the reader through this process with such grace, humor, and utter transparency that I couldn't help but see my own faith journey in hers. A refreshing, hopeful book from an expert storyteller."

—JASON BOYETT, author of *O Me of Little Faith*

"Addie Zierman's unflinching candor and tender vulnerability make *When We Were on Fire* a must-read memoir. I ached for the wholesome, eager young girl seeking to serve God with all her heart, and wept for her—for all of us—who have experienced that particular keening heart-break of being consumed by zeal. Addie walks through fire and still comes through shining with hope."

—ELIZABETH ESTHER, author of *Girl at the End of the World*

"Addie Zierman is a poet with a lion's heart. *When We Were on Fire* is a memoir of such sophisticated and witty grace, it reads as the laughing prayer of a vagabond saint. Zierman's words take root in you, grow slowly, and push outward into a ring of endless light. Would that in my own days of fire, youth groups, and See You at the Pole rallies, I had been given this book with the single word: 'Hope.'"

—PRESTON YANCEY, author of SeePrestonBlog.com

"Addie speaks for an evangelical generation who came of age in the American teen ghetto of youth group short-term mission trips and long-ings for revival, contemporary Christian music, and WWJD. Her jour-ney through the disillusionments and then her rebellion against the false boundary-markers and empty language of an "on fire" faith culminate in her ongoing journey of hope and redemption. There is a wise sadness to her words, a depth that disarms. Addie is a beautiful writer, but she's also bold and honest as she tends the wounds of consumer evangelicalism on her old self, and then bravely gathers up all these disparate pieces of the painful and lovely obsessive faith of her past with new grace and gentle strength to move forward."

—SARAH BESSEY, author of *Jesus Feminist*

"For all of us who found our way while steeped in evangelical culture, Addie has written us a love letter. Hilarious and heartfelt, passionate and poetic, her take on growing up evangelical reveals a classic coming-of-age story with an evangelical twist. Through clean and messy faith, confusion, love lost and gained, she reflects deeply on each experience with enough humility and humor to keep you turning pages through this easy and beautiful read. You will love *When We Were on Fire* from beginning to end, as did I."

—GRACE BISKIE, author of *Converge Bible Studies: Kingdom Building,* contributing author of *Talking Taboo: American Christian Women Get Frank About Faith,* and writer for DeeperStory.com and *Prodigal & Prism* magazine

"Reading *When We Were on Fire* was like reading my own story. It's an insightful, unflinching look at growing up evangelical. Addie recounts her misplaced zeal and resulting crisis of faith with humor and poignancy… ultimately discovering that a relationship with God is less about following Christian culture norms and more about following Him."

—KRISTEN HOWERTON, blogger at *Rage Against the Minivan,* and psychology professor at Vanguard University

"It's rare that a storyteller comes along with the ability to address important issues of life and faith with strength and profound openness. Addie Zierman is that kind of storyteller, and she does just that with her debut book *When We Were on Fire*. With a keen grasp on the intricacies and absurdities of Christian subculture, Addie bravely tells her story of a real, honest, and vulnerable faith that will resonate with readers of all ages. *When We Were on Fire* is a true pleasure to read."

—NISH WEISETH, author of *Speak: How Your Story Can Change the World*, and editor-in-chief at DeeperStory.com

"Addie Zierman is a master storyteller whose sharp wit is matched only by her disarming sincerity. *When We Were on Fire* introduces her as one of this generation's most promising new voices. Prepare to laugh out loud and nod along as this book delights, challenges, tickles, and inspires. For those of us working to reconcile the faith of our youth with the faith of our adulthood, it's such a joy to have a friend like Addie along for the journey."

—RACHEL HELD EVANS, author of *Evolving in Monkey Town* and *A Year of Biblical Womanhood*

"The best kind of memoir is so deeply personal that it tells a universal story. In Addie's memoir you will find funny, messy, cringe-worthy, and beautiful moments that cut close to home—those experiences that we would like to relegate to youth but in truth lurk not far beneath the surface of every phase of life. If you are weary of sanitized and teetotaling stories, and are hungry for honest and redemptive stories, then this is your story."

—ADAM S. McHUGH, author of *Introverts in the Church*

 Churchill County Library
553 S. Maine Street
Fallon, Nevada 89406
(775) 423-7581

NOV 13

Churchill County Library
553 S. Maine Street
Fallon, Nevada 89406
(775) 423-7581

When We Were on Fire

A Memoir of Consuming Faith,
Tangled Love, and Starting Over

Addie Zierman

CONVERGENT
BOOKS

WHEN WE WERE ON FIRE
PUBLISHED BY CONVERGENT BOOKS

Scripture quotations are taken from the Holy Bible, New International Version®, NIV®.
Copyright © 1973, 1978, 1984 by Biblica Inc.™ Used by permission of Zondervan. All rights
reserved worldwide. www.zondervan.com.

Details in some anecdotes and stories have been changed to protect the identities of the persons
involved.

Trade Paperback ISBN 978-1-60142-545-4
eBook ISBN 978-1-60142-546-1

Copyright © 2013 by Addie Zierman

Two small portions of this book were originally published in *Relief* journal and in *Defunct*
magazine.

Cover design by Kristopher K. Orr

Published in association with the literary agency of Janet Kobobel Grant, Books & Such, 52
Mission Circle, Suite 122, PMB 170, Santa Rosa, CA 95409. www.booksandsuch.biz.

All rights reserved. No part of this book may be reproduced or transmitted in any form or by any
means, electronic or mechanical, including photocopying and recording, or by any information
storage and retrieval system, without permission in writing from the publisher.

Published in the United States by Convergent Books, an imprint of the Crown Publishing
Group, a division of Random House LLC, New York, a Penguin Random House Company.

CONVERGENT BOOKS and its open book colophon are trademarks of Random House LLC.

Library of Congress Cataloging-in-Publication Data
Zierman, Addie.
    When we were on fire : a memoir of obsessive faith / Addie Zierman.—First Edition.
        pages cm
    ISBN 978-1-60142-545-4—ISBN 978-1-60142-546-1 (electronic) 1. Zierman, Addie.
2. Christian biography—United States. I. Title.
    BR1725.Z54A3 2013
    277.3'083092—dc23
    [B]

                                                                    2013022552

Printed in the United States of America
2013—First Edition

10 9 8 7 6 5 4 3 2 1

SPECIAL SALES
Most Convergent books are available at special quantity discounts when purchased in bulk by
corporations, organizations, and special-interest groups. Custom imprinting or excerpting can
also be done to fit special needs. For information, please e-mail SpecialMarkets@Convergent
Books.com or call 1-800-603-7051.

For Kim and Alissa,
who were there for the whole wild thing
and
For Andrew,
whose love makes me strong

Contents

Part Four: Redemption

Prologue

S o there I was. Alone at the flagpole. In the rain.

Behind me, Buffalo Grove High School loomed large and brown, its walls angling inward so that either way I looked, there was brick and glass, brick and glass. Inside, the school was just starting to flicker to life: a few lockers creaking open, slamming shut, the early students shuffling down the quiet hallways toward a new day.

I was standing outside on a small patch of grass in that netherworld between the school's entrance and the road. In front of me, the flagpole rose tall from a tiny concrete circle. The September rain fell steady and cold, but instead of a jacket, I was sporting my official See You at the Pole T-shirt: white with a barrage of reds and blues—a prayer-themed Bible verse splashed across in a zany font.

The shirts came in big packets of Christian marketing materials sent to youth pastors across the United States. In turn, they were doled out to students. Students who had promised to pray at their schools' flagpoles at seven in the morning that fourth Wednesday of September. Students like me.

It was my sophomore year, my second time to the national See You at the Pole event. My first year, I'd stepped out of our minivan and into a group of hundreds of students, all of them circling wide around the BGHS flagpole. They were pressing farther and farther out toward the brick walls, toward the road, toward the whole of the Chicago suburbs in which we lived.

I was innocent, small, white-blond. My body had not yet begun to curve into itself; I slid in and out of size-one jeans. But when I walked toward that burgeoning circle, it opened. It absorbed me. The hands of people I'd never met were grasping mine, while above us, the American flag snapped proudly in the wind. We were fourteen, fifteen, sixteen, standing up for something Great. We were holding hands, holding together God and country, faith and public education, Jesus and His disenfranchised children—the ones walking unseeing down our high school hallways.

That was the idea, anyway. That is what I imagine the founders of the event had in mind when they started it somewhere deep in Texas in 1990. And maybe in the beginning, it was. Maybe in its grass-roots days, it was honest and humble, a fusing together around the pain of classmates, schools, world.

But by the time I first attended in 1997, See You at the Pole was a trademarked term. It had a paid staff. A marketing team. A website. "You may purchase top-quality SYATP promotional material, such as videos, brochures, posters, book covers, banners, wristbands and more, at reasonable prices by calling 817.HIS.PLAN," the website advertised.

By 1997, youth pastors across the country were showing the SYATP video promo, and it was a kind of extended infomercial featuring good-looking Christian teenagers in fitted Abercrombie sweaters. The teens talked about God and about the wonderful things that had happened to them while standing in front of flagpoles for Jesus. I watched them fade in and out on the screen, these beautiful people I did not know. Their enthusiasm lodged itself somewhere deep inside of me, growing steadily, filling me with hope.

I was a freshman—insecure and unknown. This was my opportunity to be somebody. "This is your time to stand strong for your faith at the pole," the kids in the video said.

See. You. There.

— —

In retrospect, that first See You at the Pole event with its bloated circle of students stirs a feeling I can't quite place. *Pity. Compassion. Frustration. Nostalgia.* So much has happened since then. I almost can't remember what it felt like to be that girl—the one with the long blond ponytail streaking down her back. The skinny girl with the See You at the Pole T-shirt billowing in the wind. The shy one. The unsure one. I almost can't remember what it felt like to be caught in that moment, pulled into something big and important: a firestorm of prayer, a wind system capable of so much power.

What I do remember is that I was supposed to have my head bowed. I was supposed to be concentrating on Jesus, but my head was half raised, my eyes wide. I was counting the ever-growing number of students. I was trying to memorize their faces before they disappeared back into the anonymity of our two-thousand-some student body like rocks thrown back into a rolling sea.

I kept thinking, *There are* so many *of us!* And I believed in some deep part of me that if we just prayed hard enough on this one special day, something big and wild would sweep the locker-lined halls of my high school. *Revival.*

This is how I saw it: a wooden cross set up in the school foyer. People bringing their drugs and their cigarettes and their water bottles filled with stolen drags of vodka and leaving it all there. Leaving it in the hands of Jesus.

The details of the whole thing weren't totally clear to me. I'd never actually seen drugs, and though I'd heard rumors about the vodka water bottles, the idea was confusing to me. The word *bong* was not in my vocabulary. The mechanics of drug and alcohol use, the punch lines of dirty jokes and sexual innuendo—these were not things I understood. But at fourteen, I was aware of the way they separated me from Everyone Else. I was aware of the way they made me invisible while I fumbled with the combination to my locker, the words of my classmates soaring high over my head.

If they came to Jesus, these people in this school, none of that would matter anymore. We would all speak a common language. "Hey, how is your walk with God?" they would say, and they would be asking *me* and I would be able to tell them. They would want to know how I did it—

how I always kept my faith so strong. They would sit with me in the cafeteria, buy me one of those melty chocolate chip cookies from under the heat lamp, ask me about the Bible. I would answer with a knowing smile. My hair would have that glossy, magazine-model look. Everything would be different.

— —

On the wall of my basement bedroom, I had taped a newspaper article from that 1997 See You at the Pole event. The article was about another school in a nearby Chicago suburb—Prospect High School. That was where my sort-of boyfriend, Chris Jacobson, went. Where he was a senior, where he led the school Bible study, where he swaggered down the hall, chin up, buoyed by the chemical substance of his faith.

In the article's accompanying photograph, Chris stood front and center. With one hand, he held his *Student Study Bible* open, his palm steady. His other hand was caught by the shutter in midgesture, his fingers frozen in midair, forever emphasizing the point.

Around him, there was a circle much like the one I'd been standing in at that very moment at Buffalo Grove High School. But in the picture, the students were blurred beyond recognition. They were gray, fuzzy figures. They belonged to the background.

The flagpole was the point of the picture; Chris, his face intent on some Other World, he was the point. His blond hair parted in the middle and flopped bowl-cut style on either side of his head. He could almost be mistaken for a young boy if it weren't for the intensity in his face.

I spent many afternoons during my freshman year sitting on my bed, staring at that article. I memorized the picture so completely that even now, fifteen years later, when I think about Chris, this is the image that comes to mind: the muddy black-and-white photocopy, the open Bible, the floppy hair. Soon after that picture was taken, Chris took a Bic razor to his scalp and spent the rest of the year with a smooth, pink head. I don't remember why.

But when I conjure him up, I can't see it, that bald head. I see the boy with the floppy hair, the boy in the picture, the boy who was the point of it all.

— —

It was this newspaper article I was thinking about when I stepped out of our green minivan into that rainy Wednesday morning a year later. My mom leaned her head toward me as I hoisted my violin case and slung my backpack over my shoulder, the rain smacking against the green vinyl.

"No one's here," she pointed out. I followed her eyes to the empty courtyard, the flag shivering on the metal pole, the puddles gathering in the creases of the concrete.

I shrugged. "I don't care," I said. "I'm still going to do it."

"Are you sure?" she asked, her voice rising a little with concern. The feathery ends of her hair were still stuck to her head where the pillow had pressed them overnight.

"I'm sure, Mom," I said impatiently. I grabbed a pile of green fluorescent fliers off the dash. They announced the start of the school Bible study in loud fonts, big lettering. I'd planned to hand them around the circle to herald the new school year, the new Buffalo Grove High School Bible Study, which would be led by me and my two best friends, Kim and Alissa. I jammed the fliers into my backpack between two textbooks.

"Okay…," Mom said uncertainly. "Well, have fun."

I walked alone to the flagpole, stood in front of it with my head bowed so that all I could see was the place where the pole disappeared into the concrete base. I put my violin case on the ground, and the water slid over its black lid and collected along the metal clasps.

And here is my secret: *I wanted this.*

I wanted the empty courtyard, the chance to be a solitary figure at the pole. To be the only one bold enough, brave enough, passionate enough to stand in the rain for Jesus.

I was fifteen, foggy on the difference between alone and lonely, unaware of how close they were, of how the former could slip so easily into the latter. I was desperate for independence and distinction. I stood tall. I looked down.

I imagined the camera crew from the *Daily Herald* pulling up alongside me in a van. I saw myself the focus of a camera lens: profile view. Me, head bowed as the water beat down on me, as it trailed down my face. The picture would show the water clinging crystalline to my closed lashes. Behind me, there would be empty space where you'd expect to see others, and their absence would be a tribute to my singularity, my sacrifice: a lone figure, deep in prayer, while the flag slapped wet above.

I stood, shifted, waited, the puddles growing deeper under my Payless tennis shoes. The rain pattered against my hair, making my ponytail heavy on my neck.

If I prayed that day, it was in short, unfocused statements—*Lord, please do something great in our school*—repeated again and again, leaving my mind free to listen to the sound of car doors closing behind me and feet shuffling toward the front entrance. It left me space to wonder about the passing students: who they were, what they were thinking as they noticed me, standing there with rain removing my makeup in streaks. Did they know why I was there? Would they ask me about it? (*Lord, please do something great in our school.*)

I pictured myself walking sopping wet into my first class, the bottoms of my green, flared jeans darkened by water. I pictured my classmates turning to look at me—the chatter stilled for a moment, the momentum of the morning coming to a full stop. (*Lord, please do something great in our school.*)

What I did not know then, could not see, was that the entry hall of the high school had filled up with a widening circle of students. They were pressing against the walls, blocking the doors to the stairwell, holding each other's hands, praying out loud.

It never occurred to me that the location of the event would be changed for the weather, and it wasn't until five minutes before the bell that Kim came running out, her windbreaker held over her head like an umbrella, to wave me inside.

"We couldn't figure out where you were!" she told me later as I stood by my locker, dripping, my SYATP shirt clinging formless and uncomfortable to my skin. Kim leaned against a locker while Alissa straightened out the pile of crinkled fliers I'd pulled from my bag. "I couldn't believe it when I finally looked outside and saw you just standing there."

The look on her face was not admiration. It was pity. It was as if she understood what I could not. There were two places to stand: a flagpole and a crowded hallway. I could only see one.

I thought I was choosing something extraordinary.

I thought this would all turn out differently.

Part One

Obsession

One

To invite Jesus into one's heart: A foundational prayer that forms the basis of the evangelical conversion experience. In this prayer, a person confesses her sins and accepts Jesus Christ as Lord and Savior. In exchange, she receives the assurance of heaven and the promise of God's presence and involvement in daily life.

You were born into a world within a world. *Evangelicalism*. It is spinning on its own axis, powered by its own sun—the radiance of God's glory bright above you.

You were born to the Church People, the first baby in the Young Marrieds' Sunday school class at Deerbrook Evangelical Free Church. You were something of a mascot—the blue-eyed, dimpled dream of every young couple—and you were passed from one set of waiting arms to another, plastered weekly with kisses.

Of course, this is not the kind of thing you'd remember, but you have a distinct feeling that it left its own kind of impression on you...this unearned love bestowed on you from birth by a group of people. Church People. Sunday school husbands and wives, who touched your face with their hands one moment and folded them in prayer the next.

What you *do* remember are coloring books filled with Bible illustrations. The Red Sea splitting in two, waves shooting up on either side so Moses could lead the people through. David, the shepherd, tending his flock. Jesus standing on a hill with loaves in one hand and fish in the other. You were filling the outlines of these pictures with color until they sprang to life in your imagination. In the background, Psalty the Singing Songbook sang praise songs to Jesus from the cassette player.

You remember *Sesame Street* and *Mister Rogers' Neighborhood,* of course, but you also watched *Flying House,* a Christian cartoon featured on Pat Robertson's *700 Club.* You remember the theme song, that beginning number where some kids stumble into a creepy mansion and then find themselves flying through space and time, turning up a little bewildered in the middle of various Bible stories.

You grew up praying out loud every night before bed, your mom at your bedside, your body tucked tight under that Bible story quilt your aunt made. And then one day, you prayed The Prayer, and you were five. You'd just had your first nightmare about hell.

In the dream, fire had been everywhere around you, and Satan was there. You couldn't, upon waking, remember the exact look of him, but you will never forget the *feel* of him: a distinctly overwhelming kind of evil. The sound of his laugh reverberated off the walls of your empty bedroom, and you woke into it, sweaty and shaking.

You ran to your parents' room that morning, and you crawled, crying, into their bed. You can still remember the weight of fear as it pressed in on you and those comforting words about God and about heaven and about Love. Your mom prayed The Prayer then, and you repeated after her, a small bell, echoing.

Dear Jesus, Please come into my heart and take all of my sins away.

Years later, you will remember only the faint outline of this moment. The general tenor of it. But you will hold it in your pocket like a touchstone; you will touch it with the tips of your fingers when you feel unsure. After all, so much depends on this prayer. So much flows from "into my heart"…a kingdom ushered into your small soul. A world within a world.

You grew up attending Deerbrook Evangelical Free Church, a great brown building at the northwest edge of the Chicago suburbs. It had a steeple with a bell that had been broken for as long as you could remember. To you, the extended wings of the church looked like arms open wide.

Your parents met at Deerbrook one morning when the Sunday school class they were both visiting formed groups based on birth dates, and as luck—or God—would have it, his was March 2nd, hers the 4th. They'd gone there ever since, the life of that church fused irrevocably with the beginnings of their own story. In some ways, Deerbrook felt more like home than any house you ever lived in.

You explored every hallway, every corridor. You hid beneath the stairwells, ran wild through the sanctuary, ducking underneath the pews, staring up at stained glass. You watched a variety of gentle teachers stick paper Bible characters to felt boards, and you knew them, and they knew you, and this was your place. These were your people.

In a chorus of other five-year-olds, you learned to sing loud on Sunday mornings: short, sweet songs about Jesus and Father Abraham and the B-I-B-L-E. You learned to believe the words of those songs, as simple and complex as the palm of your own small hand.

By third grade, you could recite all sixty-six books of the Bible in the correct order. You'd get a little tripped up around the end of the Old Testament with its similar and confusing book names: *Jonah, Micah, Nahum, Habakkuk. Zephaniah, Haggai, Zechariah, Malachi.* But you knew them like landmarks on a well-worn map. You learned to find them fast in the tissuey pages of your children's Bible.

You were poised for Sunday morning Sword Drills, when a teacher read aloud a reference to a Bible verse and promised a prize to the first one to find it in his Bible. You can still remember what it felt like at the edge of that metal folding chair, fingers suspended over your Bible, your heart loud in your chest. You can still conjure the feel of delicate pages between your fingers as you flipped *fast, faster, fastest,* your lips moving as you re-cited: "Genesis, Exodus, Leviticus, Numbers…"

—•—

At night, Bible lessons played from cassette tapes that came in the mail from your grandma. You'd lie on your bed, tucked into the covers, washed and pajamaed, and you'd listen to a story.

The one that sticks in your mind goes like this:

There is a boy. It is his birthday, and a sledding party has been planned.

His mom is making a pot of hot cocoa, and on the table she sets a bowl of big, puffy, white marshmallows.

"Now, don't eat these marshmallows," the mother says. "They're for the party."

And then she leaves the boy alone. In the room. With the marshmallows.

And after all, it is his birthday.

Of course, he eats one.

And then the party begins. The guests arrive, and everyone goes sledding. When they come inside, pink-cheeked and happy, the cocoa is steaming hot. Everyone gets a full mug with a big marshmallow floating and melting on top.

When the boy comes to get his cup, however, his mother looks at him sadly. "I'm sorry, sweetie," she says. "There aren't enough marshmallows for you to have one."

What you were meant to learn is that it always catches up with you. *Sin*. A marshmallow stolen in the dark hum of an empty kitchen means *consequences* later, even on your *birthday*, even if you're sorry, even if no one saw you do it.

You learned it well, this lesson, and the truth of it pulsed with your heartbeat whenever you even thought about doing something wrong. You were learning to live by the God-light in your heart, learning the cost of disobedience, learning that your actions had the power to please Jesus or to disappoint Him.

And oh, how you wanted Him to be happy with you.

There was a picture of Him on your copy of *The Children's Living*

Bible, and He had short black hair and a tidy beard. You could see the dimple creased into His cheek as He looked down at a white lamb, held safe in His arms.

It was through 1970s-era illustrations like this that you first encountered God: well-groomed and fun-loving. On the inside cover of your Bible, Jesus stood at the seaside with a bunch of good, blue-eyed children in jeans and T-shirts. Overhead, sea gulls winged wide circles in the sky.

However wrongly imagined or inaccurately portrayed, the picture *spoke* to you, and you immediately loved this version of Jesus. He was walking across a field in His white tunic and red sash, His sandaled feet frozen in midstep, and you were the fair-skinned child next to Him. You were skinny, rosy-cheeked, maybe seven years old. You were handing Him flowers you'd picked from the meadow. He was smiling down at you as if you were His lamb, as if He'd never loved anything more than He loved you right then.

━ ━

For six years of Wednesday nights, you attended Awana Clubs at your church. While the kids at school were at Boy or Girl Scouts or soccer practice, you were learning Bible verses from an evangelical nonprofit that had been thrumming in Christian circles since the 1950s. You started out in the Awana Cubbies program, with its friendly teddy bear mascot and its small, lovely truths. *God created the world. God loves me.*

In early elementary school, you graduated to Sparks, where the mascot was a chipper-looking lightning bug. He wore a red hat, and he represented the Light of Christ that you were meant to hold inside of you. You were a *spark,* friendly and bright. You were made to light up the world.

You remember the Sparks uniform, a red vest that you wore over your T-shirts on Wednesday nights, and you remember the bronze, silver, and gold plastic crowns pinned to the left side. You remember the weight

and feel of the workbooks, Bible verse after Bible verse listed inside, waiting to be memorized. After you could say a certain number of them aloud
perfectly, you'd get a tiny plastic jewel to put into the crown on your vest.

The first boy you ever *liked* wore a Sparks vest to school sometimes,
and his crowns were full of jewels, indicating successful memorization of
so many verses. His name was Ben, and he was a little bit nerdy. He wore
thick glasses and sported a blond buzz cut. He wasn't particularly funny
or clever. But he had a Sparks vest that was *filled* with crowns and jewels,
and he wore it boldly in your public school class.

It was this combination of bravery and accomplishment that drew
you in and made you decide to like him. You *chose* it. Chose him. He
would be the first in a line of boys you would love simply for their faith.
The strength of it. The boldness of it. The glittering of all of those jewels
in all of those crowns.

———

You spent your growing-up years walking by a map of the world that was
stretched out on the wall in Deerbrook's foyer. Around it, the support-
card photos of missionaries extended, tied to their countries with long,
taut strings. You knew their faces by heart, these people, but you had
never met most of them. They were gone, far-flung across the world, living exotic lives for Jesus.

When the missionary from Africa came to talk to your Sunday
school class, he brought a bag made from a monkey skin and the long,
papery skin of a python. "The python is one of the biggest snakes in the
world," the missionary said that day. "He could eat you in one swallow."

You couldn't imagine it, but that didn't make it less fearful. You were
from the well-ordered Chicago suburbs, where pythons existed only behind thick glass at Brookfield Zoo. You could press your nose and breathe
circles of fog onto the window, but in the end, the snake's habitat was
definitively separated from your world of minivans and raincoats and
thin McDonald's cheeseburgers wrapped in crinkly yellow paper.

At the front of the room, the missionary man slung that monkey bag around the chair by its tail-turned-purse-strap. "Now," he said, "who would like to touch a snakeskin?"

The kids in your Sunday school class clamored to the front of the room, but you remained seated. You understood, even then, that missionaries did important work, that there were people in the world who did not know about Jesus, about sin, about heaven and hell. But you were frightened, already, of the faraway unknown. Jaguars creeping dark and hungry along tree branches, fish that would eat the flesh right off your arm, snakes so big they could swallow you whole.

Already, you feared that God might want to send you to those places. You'd been in Sunday school long enough to know how the story goes: the voice of God comes down from the sky and asks you to go where you don't want to go, to do what you don't want to do. And you have to do it anyway.

You did not touch the missionary's artifacts that day. Was it just about the unfamiliar snake scales that you feared? Or did you avoid touching the skin because you knew you would be marked for it—the missionary life? That God would ask you to go, and you would have to listen, or you could end up punished, Jonah-style, in the belly of some whale?

Did you pray in those fearful folding-chair moments? Beg God not to make you a missionary? Or do you only imagine it now, all these years later?

—— · ——

Year by year, you grew into it—this faith. This world.

One day in your tenth year, the communion plate went by, and you reached to take the body, the blood. There is no First Communion ritual in the evangelical faith; you take communion when you feel you understand what it means and when your parents think you're old enough. But that morning, your dad passed the tray over your head, and you watched it disappear toward the end of the aisle. You watched the people with their broken bits of cracker, *body of Christ,* and for the first time ever at church, you felt isolated. Left out.

That night, you sat on the front stoop with your dad, and he asked you what you thought *communion* meant. You remember the darkening sky, the magnolia tree beginning to lose its leaves.

You mumbled something about Jesus and the cross. You crossed your arms and looked at your feet, irritated at him for making you prove yourself. A breeze lifted the air, and you could smell Old Spice deodorant and wintergreen Certs.

Your dad was not the one in the family who usually talked about the spiritual stuff. Usually that fell to your mom, who moved so naturally in the language of God. Your dad seemed more comfortable in quiet and mystery: An open leather Bible. A glass of red wine.

But that night, he was slow and deliberate in the conversation, making lots of space for silence. He explained communion, and you could sense the gravity of it, the weight of that holy meal. You nodded as he spoke, and you stared down at your black stretch pants, which had gotten loose around the knees over the course of the day.

And it wasn't so much the broken communion crackers you wanted. You wanted him to see you as you saw yourself: old enough, capable. Ready to reach forward and take your faith into your own two hands.

You waited for him to give that final, approving nod. The one that meant you were allowed to sit at the grownup table. To take the bread and the tiny plastic cup of grape juice with careful fingers. To drink it all the way down. When he finally nodded, you smiled and slipped your arm through his. The two of you sat silent on the step, the night falling still and quiet around you.

--- • ---

And, remember, you were *born into this.* You asked Jesus into your heart, and you belonged to the Church People who had known you forever, who loved you like their own. You understood they weren't perfect, but you believed they were *good,* united in the most important ways, full to the brim with God's great love, spilling over.

Remember that first jarring moment you understood that the world was divided?

Remember Amy Grant?

She was the darling of evangelicalism, the first contemporary Christian musician to score a platinum record and show the world that evangelicals, too, could achieve excellence in the arts. She was also your mom's *favorite.* One afternoon, she transferred all of her old Amy Grant records onto cassette tapes so you have copies of your own. You looked at each of the old album covers while the record spun and the cassette recorded. You remember thinking that Amy Grant was the most beautiful person you'd ever seen. Her hair hung long and crimped around her face. Her eyes were big and brown and nothing like yours.

You memorized all of the words to "Father's Eyes." You sang it in the shower, while you lathered Pantene Pro-V into your hair. You wondered if God's eyes and Amy Grant's eyes looked the same. You wondered if having your Father's eyes would make you beautiful like Amy Grant.

Then *Heart in Motion* hit the record stands—Amy Grant's mainstream debut. On the CD jacket, she wore a red crushed velvet, baby doll dress. She looked hipper, sleeker. She didn't look at the camera the way she did on the old albums. Instead, she looked down, away, two curly tendrils escaping her updo and falling over her face.

It was your favorite CD of all time. You spent hours in your best friend Dana's basement, choreographing a complicated gymnastics routine to "Baby Baby." You wore matching unitards with a starburst of colors splashed across the chest. Somewhere in the middle of the routine, Dana flipped you over her back and you landed with a great flourish.

You learned the word *mainstream* the day "Baby Baby" came on the car radio, and your mom let it slip that the evangelicals were less than enthusiastic about the new album. It had to do with a shift in focus from *sacred* to *secular,* from praise to pop, from *Christian* to *mainstream.*

The shift toward *mainstream* had to do with lyrics that were largely about starlight and Galileo. About parking lots and about being in love… but not really all that much about the Father's eyes anymore.

Your mom sighed and drove under the flowering branches of Cottonwood Road. She shook her head at the silliness of the whole thing, but you stared out the window, silent, thoughtful. You were born to a world within a world, and suddenly you could see marked boundaries. You could see that there was *in here* and there was *out there* and between them, there was a yawning chasm. You could see that it was big enough to swallow you whole.

‣ ‣

By the end of your sixth-grade year, you could really only half remember that moment when you prayed The Prayer. It had been so long ago, and everything about those early days had become a little fuzzy in your mind. You spent a lot of time worrying that it had never actually happened.

That summer, you attended Bible camp in the backwoods of Wisconsin, where you made Shrinky Dinks and rode horses and turned a dark, mosquito-pocked kind of happy. You sang loud, wild songs about God's love at morning and evening rallies. You bought fistfuls of Lemonheads at evening Canteen while the sun set over Peter's Lake.

On the last night of camp, you sat in a large, outdoor amphitheater, and the only light came from that raging bonfire. The worship team came to the stage in jeans and T-shirts to strum softly on their guitars, and the speaker said, "I'd like everyone to bow your heads and close your eyes. Now, if there is anyone here who hasn't asked Jesus into your heart, this is the moment. Come down now."

You lowered your head and placed your hands on your knees. You could feel the sleek blond hairs stand up as the cool summer wind whipped against your legs. Dana had started shaving her legs, and you couldn't stop noticing how different your knees looked side by side. You wondered if you should start shaving too.

"Don't be ashamed," the speaker said. "This is the greatest moment of your life, and we are all here to celebrate with you." You could hear the crackle of the fire and Dana's breath, steady, easy, bored. Then the rustling began. A little shifting. A few footsteps. Your eyes peeked open just a slit, and you looked to see if it was anyone you knew.

More footsteps. More dirty tennis shoes were walking past your half-closed eyes, down the stairs toward the platform.

You started to think, *I wonder if I should be going.*

It was dark, and you were trying to picture that moment when you asked Him into your heart…but you couldn't. And your best friend, who you thought was born again already, had gotten up. She was shuffling toward the bonfire, and you were pretty sure you belonged to Jesus. But what if you were wrong?

Here under the cooling summer air and the evergreen trees, *Saved* was a moment, a once-and-for-all kind of thing, and what if you'd made yours up entirely?

You stood, walked to the front, said it one more time. Just to be sure.

➤ ━

Junior high began, and you had become an expert at the art of disappearing.

You'd learned long ago the politics of *belonging* and *not belonging.* You'd known it ever since the girls in your fifth-grade class gathered around glossy, signed photos of the pop band New Kids on the Block. When you tried to get a look, they glanced at you sideways.

"Are you in the Official NKOTB Fan Club?" one of them asked, eyes narrowed.

"No…"

"Then, sorry. You can't see. Only official members allowed." They'd shrugged then—nothing to be done, fan club rules binding—and then they'd moved to the other side of the playground to sit in the grass and sigh over boys.

So you learned to bring a book and to create a vacuum of silence in your head. At recess, you'd find a secluded corner, close enough to the dumpsters that no one would usually bother you. You could smell the damp remains of old cafeteria pizza as you read.

When the boys' dodge ball started edging nearer and nearer your quiet spot, you learned to walk and read simultaneously. Every day, you read/walked the periphery of the soccer fields during the agonizing thirty-minute lunch recess. On the far end of the field, there were three tall trees, and you imagined they were waiting for you, they would miss you if you didn't visit, they were your friends. You ached for after school, when you could get on your bike and pedal the six blocks to Dana's house—Dana, who went to a different elementary school. Dana, your only real friend.

And at age eleven, you didn't know the specifics, but you knew you *didn't fit*. At eleven, it was possible to already know so much about loneliness.

Then junior high began, and for you, it came as a gift.

On that first Sunday of the new school year, you walked into the junior high youth group room with its ripped donated couches and its photo-covered walls. You were shaking with the anxiety of it all, curled small on the ragged couch.

And then, something unbelievable happened.

They absorbed you.

Two eighth-grade girls sat down next to you *on purpose.* They looked at you with their toothpaste-ad smiles, and they said their names and asked yours. One of them touched the end of your braid. "I just love your hair!" she said kindly, and for you at age twelve, those words felt weighty and important, fragile with tentative hope.

You who had learned to disappear were suddenly *seen,* and the world was entirely altered. And if it hadn't been for that moment—those girls—who knows what would have become of your faith? You were an odd-shaped piece, and in one swift moment of kindness, you felt yourself click into place.

—•—

From there, Jesus became your *thing,* your own kind of extracurricular activity. You'd found your safe place, and you stayed there, burrowing deeper and deeper into it. You had God. You had Jesus the way other kids had soccer or drama or choir. You had youth group pizza parties and bike trips and weekend retreats. Christian CDs and Christian concerts and that Cooper Junior High Bible Study you'd started yourself.

You found yourself moving closer and closer to the fluorescent pink glow of nineties evangelical youth culture. And as you did, you noticed Dana slowly retreating from it, backing away into places you could not follow.

The differences were small at first. While you were listening to Christian rock bands and memorizing DC Talk's pro-abstinence song, "I Don't Want It," Dana was cranking up the volume on Alanis Morissette's *Jagged Little Pill.* She was singing along extra loud to the dirty parts.

You'd plastered your bedroom walls with Bible verses and one or two posters of your celebrity crush, Jonathan Taylor Thomas. Hers was covered in ripped-out articles from *Seventeen* magazine about how to know if you're a good kisser.

That summer, you went with your parents on a church mission trip to teach English in the Czech Republic; Dana stayed home and learned how to smoke tea bags.

She came over one day shortly after you came home, and you watched as she took the DC Talk CD off your dresser. "I can't believe you listen to this shit," she said, tossing it onto a pile of laundry on the floor. You were shaken by the way she'd said that word—*shit*—by how small those four letters made you feel.

"Anyway," she said, "I decided I'm not coming back to Cooper in the fall."

"What? Why?"

She didn't look at you. Instead, she skimmed the titles of the CDs lined up on the dresser, ran her fingers along their spines. The Newsboys' *Going Public*, Michael W. Smith's *Change Your World*, Jars of Clay's self-titled debut.

"My friend Iris goes to this private school, and she says all the guys there are really hot," Dana said absently. "So I think I should go there. God, don't you have *any* good music?"

Years later, when you think about Dana, you'll remember this moment. You'll wonder why you didn't press the issue, why you didn't try to figure out the real reason behind the unexpected school transfer. It must have been propelled by something deeper than boys, but you were so shocked and hurt, and your ears were pulsing with all that Christian rock.

You never actually heard the pain in her voice as she said, "Look, it's not a big deal. I just want to leave."

— —

Dana left, and God provided a new best friend. A Believer.

Her name was Alissa, and you met her in drama class, where you discovered you had the same CD collection and the same long, unstyled hair. You spent the rest of junior high school writing notes to each other in a notebook labeled *Español*, passing it back and forth in the hallway between classes.

You were fantasizing about your shared crushes, Jonathan Taylor Thomas and Devon Sawa, planning a double wedding and a lavish cruise ship vacation. And when you weren't doing that, you were coleading the Cooper Junior High Bible study. Every now and then, you accidentally wore matching outfits to school.

On infinite summer days, you rode your bikes from her house on Tanglewood to Earthen Vessels, the local Christian bookstore. Depending on how bored you were and how heavy the July humidity hung in the air, you could spend hours there, wandering. Picking up and putting down.

You found yourself intoxicated by all those *products*. You started with a Jesus fish necklace and worked your way up to T-shirts that said things like *Go Against the Flow* and *Life Is Short. Pray Hard.* In the background, the Newsboys' hit song, "Shine," played on the speaker system, loud and quiet all at once, and it became a kind of anthem in your heart.

You bought, for twenty-five cents apiece, wallet-sized cards featuring graphically enhanced Bible verses, which you taped to your wall or glued to school notebooks along with generous amounts of puffy paint and glitter. Book by pastel-covered book, you collected the entirety of a Christian teen romance series featuring Christy Miller and her Jesus-loving, surfer boyfriend. You traced the delicate silver orbs of purity rings and paged through Christian bridal magazines, and you began to develop a concept of Christian relationships that was entirely pink and swirly.

You noticed again and again a display of mustard seeds in vacuumed-sealed packets. If it weren't for the label, you would've thought the packages empty—the specks of seed were so small you could barely see them there, wedged into the bottom corners of the plastic.

You'd read about mustard seeds in your *Teen Life Application Study Bible.* Jesus said that if you had faith even as small as this seed, you could tell a mountain to move, and it would. The thought made you brave. You thought, *Surely I have more faith than that.*

It felt so big to you, that fire in your heart. It filled your body, gave you a sort of buoyancy and belonging. A sense of purpose.

Week after week, you plunked your baby-sitting money down on the counter, and you fed that small flame in your heart with one Christian product after another.

The God-fire grew big and hot and wild, and your whole world began to glow with it.

It raged in your heart, and before you knew it, you were entirely consumed.

Two

WWJD: An acronym for What Would Jesus Do?, a question-turned-fad in the late nineties, when the initials began to appear on cloth bracelets everywhere. It became a motto for evangelical Christians, who challenged one another to obey the Word of God in every decision by consistently asking themselves, "What would Jesus do?"

What is on that guy's lip?" Alissa asked in a whisper, staring up at the wall-mounted television in the corner of Mr. Stein's biology classroom.

"I think it's a caterpillar," Kim said, leaning in. She wore a baggy sweatshirt, and red flyaway hairs were drifting away from her ponytail in the morning static. Our small desks were crammed as close as possible, our backpacks slung on the floor next to us.

It was six thirty on a Wednesday morning. Freshman year of high school. The classroom smelled of ammonia and chalk, and the TV was the only source of light.

We were at our school's morning Bible study group, and we'd just watched the introduction to a documentary called *Hell's Bells: The Dangers of Rock 'N' Roll:* fans screaming and swaying, the lead singer of Fleetwood Mac dancing, convulsing, out of control on the stage.

The host, Eric Holmberg, had just sauntered onto the screen. He had a long brown mullet, and what was on his lip was a thick, ugly mustache.

"Definitely a caterpillar," I agreed without turning my head from what was shaping up to be the video equivalent of a terrible car wreck.

Eric Holmberg sat down on a stool in a room that looked like a music studio. He seemed to be in his early forties and trying very hard to look cool. "The purpose of this film is to take you on a journey to the heart of rock 'n' roll," he said.

"You'll discover what it can do to an egg." He held one up in front of the speaker behind him—*crack*—and then continued, "Your head. Your life. And your eternal soul."

"Rock music just killed that egg," Kim said, which gave us a case of the giggles and then a *look* from Susan, the Buffalo Grove High School Bible study leader. We looked down at our desks and tried to stifle our laughter.

The school Bible study met here every Wednesday morning, supervised by Mr. Stein while he graded biology tests. The Bible study was led by Susan, a thick-bodied senior who wore a letter jacket at all times and did not smile. Usually a half-dozen students showed up, but this morning, it was pretty sparse: just the three of us and Scary Susan.

Alissa and I had met Kim during the first week of high school. When she came to our lunch table, I'd noticed her blue WWJD bracelet immediately. I'd been desperately excited to see it, to find someone else who loved Jesus enough to bind the letters to her wrist. "I like your bracelet," I'd said, flashing my own rainbow wristband at her in solidarity. And that was that: She was our Third. Sisters in Christ. Friends forever.

The three of us were bonded by our faith. Known for it. We weren't as strange as the girls who walked around school with Beanie Babies draped over their heads, but we were still weird. *Religious.* Floating through the hallways in a bubble.

We believed that we were "going against the flow" on purpose—for Jesus—but really, we were never in the flow. We were a little out of sync with our peers…as freshmen we looked decidedly like seventh graders.

Our hair hung in ponytails or long and limp at our shoulders. We wore our T-shirts and sweatshirts baggy. None of us had totally figured out how to tweeze our eyebrows yet.

"How old do you think this movie is?" Kim asked under her breath.

"Mid-eighties?" I ventured. It was 1997. Mullets were out; mustaches like this one were categorically reserved for child molesters.

"That is one nasty haircut," Alissa whispered.

"I know." I zipped up my sweatshirt.

"So wrong," Kim agreed.

We were quiet for a minute while Eric Holmberg decoded a secret message from one of the rock 'n' roll albums in question. "Did you hear that?" he asked. "It said, 'The brainwashed do not know they are brainwashed.'" He looked meaningfully at the camera and waited a moment for the message to sink in.

"Oy," I said.

"It's so *early*." Alissa put her head on the desk and her long brown hair fell over her face. "Just so early for this."

And this was not how we imagined high school Bible study: a dark, empty classroom; a video about music we didn't own, didn't like; music that frankly scared us a little with its angry, screaming lyrics.

We imagined our school Bible study would be a sunlit corridor: open, round, filled with cute, Jesus-loving boys who would date us, take us to prom, marry us. We imagined that it would be our niche, and we kept attending just in case it ever changed. We kept going because we felt we should and because one day, we would take over and wrestle it into what we wanted it to be.

The screen faded into a montage of live performances: Pink Floyd, Prince, Billy Idol, Madonna. One of the guys from Kiss stuck out a long, red tongue. The lyrics to AC/DC's "Hells Bells" flashed across the screen, and it was the end of Part 1.

Susan peeled herself up off the tiled floor where she'd been lying since the middle of the movie. She yawned. "What'd you guys think?"

Alissa, Kim, and I looked at her and nodded mutely. We were too scared of her to say that this movie had no bearing on our lives and that we hated it. We didn't know how to say that the rock stars on this documentary may have been cultural icons—but not in the culture we understood, the one we belonged to. The culture where our matching bracelets begged the question "What Would Jesus Do?" and the answer had nothing to do with music and everything to do with how we walked in the hallways: different, unique, speaking our own special language.

"Well," Susan said, "it's a five-part series, so we'll be working on this for the next several weeks. See you guys next Wednesday."

Kim and I looked at each other with wide eyes. Alissa made a gun from her fingers and shot herself dead.

Three

Yours in Christ: A phrase often used in the closing of a letter from one believer to another. Meant to highlight the unity of life in Christ—how in some mystical way, Christians become extensions of one another, one body moving in the world.

There was really no choice but to date him, to sort-of date him, to be his almost-not-quite girlfriend, to be *his,* his forever, xoxo. There was nothing to do but doodle in curly handwriting on the pages of my algebra notebook: *Addie + Chris = Love.* Hearts blooming bubbly along the margins. It was always going to start this way.

To begin with, he was a senior. Tall, blond, blue-eyed. A varsity baseball player in those white pants with the blue stripe down the side. In that white shirt, *Knights* sprawling navy across his broad chest as he jogged in from the outfield. The brim of a baseball cap curled over his forehead, his eyes grinning at me beneath it.

To begin with, he was perfect.

He was a senior, and I was a freshman. *He was a senior…*and I had been waiting to fall in love since the seventh grade. Maybe even before. Maybe since fourth grade when I spent the year gazing across the classroom at Richard Gillian, or since the fifth grade and Dave Sibley. Or sixth grade, when Carl Mills gave me that little square Valentine's Day card with a mad professor on it. The professor's eyes were bugging out of his head and little hearts were exploding everywhere. *Mad about you,* the card had said.

At any rate, I'd spent the majority of junior high waiting for something like this to happen to me. I was listening to Mariah Carey, who was not a Christian recording artist per se, but whose sappy songs perfectly mirrored my own preteen angst as I lay in bed at night, imagining what I'd say to Jonathan Taylor Thomas when I met him at last.

I was combing my long blond hair again and again. I was frequenting Randhurst Mall with Alissa, clicking through the metal racks of clothes at a shop called Rave with the other preteens, pulling crushed velvet baby doll dresses over my stick-straight figure in the dressing room stalls, wondering if *this one* would make the boys finally notice me.

In my closet, I'd stashed a copy of *The Get-Him Guide: The Ultimate Flirting Manual,* which I'd seen in one of those black-and-white, full-page advertorials at the back of *Seventeen* magazine at Dana's house. The ad pictured a beautiful girl plastered against the muscular arm of a beautiful boy, a boy who reminded me a little bit of Zack Morris in *Saved by the Bell*—bleached-blond hair sticking gelled from his head and that same endearing smile—and I sent away for the guide immediately. I believed high school would be like that teen sitcom, and I wanted to know what to do to be like Kelly Kapowski: head cheerleader, girlfriend to Zack, my personal heroine. I wanted to know what I had to do to be loved.

Anyway, I sent the cash in the mail, even though I knew that was generally a bad idea. I couldn't imagine asking my mom to write out a check so I could buy *The Get-Him Guide*. I had a feeling this wasn't the sort of book that nice Christian girls ordered. But I also had a feeling that inside the book were the secrets I desperately wanted to know.

The total cost was $9.75, but I stuck a crisp ten dollar bill in the envelope so that no telltale quarters would roll along the bottom, giving me away. I rushed home from school for five weeks in a row in order to intercept the book when it came. When it finally did, I carried the heavy manila envelope downstairs to my bedroom where I ripped it open furiously, and there it was: *The Get-Him Guide* in all of its glory.

I read the *Guide* late into the night, read it with a flashlight underneath the covers of my twin bed, the wide circle of light illuminating the magic world of teenage girls and teenage boys and flirting.

When I finished reading, I crept out from under the covers and stood in front of my mirror, looking at myself in the faint glow of the moon streaking through the bedroom window. And I was *ready*.

— —

I've scoured the Internet for traces of this flirting book. No luck. I might have the name wrong, but I feel sure that the phrase *Get Him* is in the title somewhere. I remember the cover being black and white and cheap-looking, but I'd like to hold it in my hands again. I'd like to remember now, as an adult, what it felt like to be thirteen, so intoxicated by the idea of romance, by the silvery sheen of it, by the way it glimmered like imagined water pooling at the place up ahead where the road dips low, disappears.

I can only remember two bits of advice from the *Guide*. First, if you hope to get a boy's attention, you mustn't look too busy or preoccupied. If, say, you're on a bench, reading a book, you should look up every now and again. Flash a smile. Show you're Open and Available. The other thing I remember has to do with kissing. When kissing a boy, you shouldn't be afraid to let your tongue explore his mouth, the *Guide* had said. This tip remains in my memory, I imagine, because the idea of sloshing around another person's mouth grossed me out. In my imagination, my first kiss would be stardust and rosy whorls of romance, not saliva and teeth and gums.

But I can remember nothing else of the book, and I have a feeling this is not because I have forgotten, but rather because I absorbed it all instantly, a sort of inadvertent osmosis. It slipped into my psyche with a satisfying little *click,* and from then on, it was part of me. From then on, I could no longer sit on a bench for hours, lost in a good book. Every few seconds, I would have to look up and around as if to say, *Hello, boys. I'm Open. I'm Available. Look at me.*

— ● —

Chris Jacobson was one of those people with sparkle about him. I saw it right away when I stepped tentatively into the high school youth group room that first time as a freshman. I saw it when he looked up from the open Bible on his lap, from the ragged couch where he sat, when he smiled at me.

I held his gaze for a moment, looked down at my jean shorts, then quickly up again with a cautious smile. (A technique I'd learned in *The Get-Him Guide*? Quite possibly.)

That was how it started.

In the beginning, it was Subway sandwiches after church on Sundays. My family went home, but I got inside Chris's old black Toyota, which smelled like him—Aspen cologne and cats. I sat in the front seat, glancing cautiously at his profile next to me as he drummed the steering wheel and sang along to upbeat Christian songs. After a few Sundays, I was putting my feet on the dash, leaning my head back against the headrest. His hand draped casually across the back of the seat, and he sat back, legs apart, only the tips of his fingers guiding the steering wheel.

It started with e-mails sent from him during his morning study hall. "Had a great time in the Word this morning." The e-mails would describe the things he was learning from God. "What do you think?" the e-mails would ask. "What are you learning?" And before long, it evolved into phone calls. Every night the sound of the phone's ring elicited a Pavlovian exhilaration, sending me rocketing from whatever task I was currently undertaking.

In the winter, I sat in the basement stairwell or on top of the heating vent in the dark bathroom as we talked. In the spring, I pulled the phone by its long curly cord out through the back door and onto the tiny green deck. With shoes off, I'd climb onto the porch railing, his voice in my ear and the smell of new grass swirling around my skin. We could talk for hours, until the first fireflies began to flicker in the crab apple tree or until Dad looked pointedly out the screen door until I got the message.

Chris didn't *say* love at first, but one night he said, "I met a girl named Addie last summer in Australia." He was talking about his two-month mission trip to Australia, the one that set him apart as the most spiritual of us all.

"Really?" I said. "That's cool." I tried not to resent that another person with my name existed and had appeared, however briefly, in his life.

"Yeah…she was neat…but she had nothing on you."

— ◆ —

I want to clarify something here. This is not a love story. It is a story about that sneaky, subliminal moment when the trajectory of your life changes.

The Boy says about another girl, "She had nothing on you," and your chest fills with an intoxicating kind of hope. Suddenly your identity feels like a very fluid concept. You push at it with the palm of your hand, and it moves exactly where you want it to go, like putty, like clay.

So you form it around The Boy—because you want to *Get Him*. You never dream that when, years later, you go to push your identity back, it will be fixed in place. When you try to move it, it will crack beneath your fingers.

— ◆ —

His Australian mission trip was organized by Teen Mania, an evangelical teen missions organization whose goal was to spread the gospel message. In those days, they used a drama about a ship and pirates and a Good Captain to share the story of Jesus in faraway countries.

On his team, Chris played the role of Captain, every day donning blue pants and a white shirt and the weighty responsibility of becoming the symbol of Jesus Christ for countless nonbelievers.

Once, he lay in the grass under the vast Australian sky, tired from the day's performances, unsure if he could go on. Then, suddenly, he noticed the Southern Cross above him—a constellation visible only in the Southern Hemisphere. Four bright stars set in the sky to form the Latin cross. "I just knew right then that I would never lead a normal life," he told me in an awed whisper. "God had something Big in store for me."

These were the sort of things that happened to Chris. He led Bible studies and he led prayer groups and he led people in the Prayer of Salvation. The binding on his Bible was falling off from so much opening and closing, the words marked by his underlines, the margins heavy with his notes.

When he talked about faith, he used words like *revival,* words like *spiritual battle* and *prayer warrior* and *sacrifice.* He signed his e-mails and letters with the phrase *Consumed by the Call.*

Next to Chris's, my faith felt flimsy. It was real, but it was small, fragile, emotional.

But Chris said, "No regrets," and Chris said, "We only have one life," and I was fourteen. It sounded so good. I was watching his life, this high school senior who saw signs from God etched in the sky. His life was an arrow, sharp and straight. It pointed to a future unalterable, a future infinitely more exciting than the one I felt myself drifting toward.

I was already into Jesus; I was growing daily more and more into Chris. So there was really no choice but to follow him, to shadow his movements, to be consumed by his call, his passion, his thoughts on God—to become *his,* to be his forever, xoxo.

I was waist deep before I ever met him. It was just a matter of going all the way in.

— ▬ ▬

Chris lived a couple of suburbs away from me, in a duplex behind a strip mall. He didn't have a backyard the way I did, only a small parking lot with a short metal fence. The lights from the mall parking lot flooded fluorescent over the back of the house, illuminating a dumpster overflow-ing and broken glass ground into the crab grass lining the walkway. In-side, the house always felt dark. It was crowded with things accumulated, things unneeded, things piled upon things, making it difficult to move around.

When he was home, Chris's dad sat in the cluttered living room with all the lights off, playing opera music on an old record player. We'd walk past him on our way to youth group, quiet so as not to break the spell.

Every morning, Chris got up early and slipped out of his house. He went to the Prospect High School gym to lift weights, to run, to push, pull, push, pull, the weights clanging and his muscles burning in his arms and legs. I thought it was about maintaining health, about fighting against a bent toward obesity that he imagined was lodged somewhere in his DNA—but now, looking back, I see that it was *all of it*. It was haunt-ing him, I see now, this fear of becoming commonplace, of disappearing into the darkness.

He was running. He was bolting—moving in the general direction of God and of vibrant faith. But in the end, he was always *running from*.

At fourteen, I didn't understand this. It didn't *look* like escape. It looked like flight, wide-winged and glorious.

I suppose this is why, midway through that first year, Chris stopped me as I was getting ready to go to Subway with him for what had become our normal Sunday tradition. "I can't," he said sadly, handing me a thick, folded letter.

"What's this?" I asked, putting my coat the rest of the way on. I took the paper in my hands and looked at it cautiously.

"Just read it." Chris gave me a fast, crushing hug and then turned away. He disappeared into the crowded fellowship hall, weaving through the chatting ladies and the running children and the men drinking black coffee, everyone milling about in the rays of sun that streaked down from the skylight.

I held the letter in my hand all the way home in my parents' minivan, my stomach knotted as my little sister and brother fought in the backseat. I waited until I was alone in my bedroom, the door closed tight, to unfold the papers and read them.

The gist was that he would be leaving for Teen Mania to become a full-time intern in August, and he didn't want to get tangled up in the sticky web of a relationship. He didn't want it to keep him from following the Lord with his full, devoted heart. He didn't think we should talk anymore, didn't think we should spend Sunday afternoons driving around in his Toyota, didn't think we should be friends. The gist was that even though we weren't really, truly, officially "dating," we should break up, and that the reason for this was God.

It was, of course, not a true breakup, but it felt true, and it was enough to set me sobbing against my pillow, enough to bring both of my parents down to my bedroom where they sat next to me on my bed. I gave them the letter because I couldn't stop crying to explain. My mom silently read the pages and then handed them wordlessly to my dad. "It'll be okay," she kept saying as she rubbed my back. Dad shook his head as he skimmed over the pages but said nothing.

It was enough to drain the color from my skin for the next few months, leaving me pale and fragile-looking. I was unsure what to do at youth group, when Chris walked purposely from person to person, asking each about his or her week while carefully avoiding my gaze. I was unsure how to cope with this sudden loss, the normal language of breakups inaccessible to me because mine was for lofty purposes: it was God's idea, this parting, this emptiness. It was as though God and Chris had talked it over, and I was left alone to cope with the decision they had reached without me.

There was no place for anger, for the stages of teenage grief to unfurl in all of their grandiose agony. Instead, I worked to bear up under it. So when, months later, Chris came back with a great wide smile and a new word from God on the matter—our relationship was okay now, a *gift* from the Father rather than a liability—all I felt was a deep surge of relief.

The only thing I knew was that I had to do whatever I could to make sure he never left again.

— ◆ —

We were running. We were running together, hand in hand toward a passionate, God-inspired future. He wanted to change the world; I wanted to be by his side when he did it. When he asked me one night on the way home from church what I wanted to do with my life, there was really only one answer to give him.

"I don't know *exactly*," I said, looking solemnly out the window. "I just know I don't want to live the normal suburban life." I paused, listened as he inhaled expectantly. "I want to do something great for the Lord."

It was as if he had been waiting for this moment to love me.

I looked at him, and he was smiling. I knew what it meant to say this. It meant opening myself to the possibility of giant python skins and monkey bags and the lonely missionary life—the one I had begged God never to give me.

But I was not thinking about that just then. I was thinking about the boy sitting next to me, about his wide smile, about the way his arms felt around me when he hugged me tight. I was thinking that I would do anything to be with him.

Chris pulled spontaneously into the tiny parking lot of a small neighborhood park. It was the only impulsive thing I can ever remember him doing. "Let's swing," he said.

We sat on the black plastic swings, kicked off from the ground. Up, up, up.

During the day, mothers brought their small children here to play. They watched them climb up ladders and scoot down slides and fall and scrape their knees. They stood guard against the busy street, and protected that magic bubble of childhood. They watched, waited, their small, normal, suburban lives marked by deep, vigilant love. And we, two evangelical teenagers, had deemed this work as something *less*. Less important. Less noble. Too commonplace to matter.

This is it, I thought. *This is finally it. I am his; I am his forever.* And there was no way to know that there was something dangerous about this kind of love. That, however unintentionally, Chris had sought me out, a girl who was submissive, compliant, unformed. That he needed my weakness the way I needed his strength. That we were in the middle of a slow fall, plummeting together like stones.

The Get-Him Guide did not warn me about this; it simply gave a formula, a technique. I thought I'd mastered it. I didn't realize that he was the one who chose me.

We sat on the swings, breathing in the almost-spring air. Chris was staring at the sky, so I stared too…looking for the Southern Cross, waiting for a sign as we pumped toward the stars.

four

Revival: A spiritual awakening, particularly regarding a group of people previously unmoved by matters of faith.

S omeone's going to see us," Alissa whispered, shifting from one foot to the other and glancing around. "They're going to think we're crazy."

"No one's going to see us," Kim groaned. Even as a freshman, she was the most rebellious of all of us. (Years later, she would be escorted out of Stonehenge for jumping the rope barrier and touching the rocks.) "Look, there's no one even here." She dropped her backpack on the floor with a heavy thud and gestured to the school cafeteria.

The lights glowed fluorescent above us, bouncing off the windows. A few students were scattered around, bent over their textbooks, but it was 6:40 in the morning. For the most part, the place was empty.

"It's fine," I agreed, pulling a small Brummel & Brown container out of my backpack. "No one cares."

The container held a couple of tablespoons of Aldi-brand vegetable oil, which we had because we were planning to "anoint" the cafeteria table. We'd heard that there was specific oil made for this task, but we didn't have any. Anyway, plain old cooking oil was what I had seen Chris use the week before.

I'd never heard of this symbolic gesture before I saw him "anoint" the door frame of the home of one of his friends before a prayer meeting. I'd watched him dip his fingers into the small dish and bring them out, shining and damp. He'd closed his eyes and touched the door frame, and it had all seemed so beautiful and so holy that I could barely catch my breath.

"The Israelites used to do this," Chris had told me that night, "when they wanted to show that something was sacred." He paused, wiped his fingers methodically on a small napkin he'd taken out of his pocket.

"Right," I'd said, as if I knew just the passage he was talking about. It was not a typically evangelical symbol, not a rite I'd ever seen performed at our church, and the newness of it made it seem extreme and powerful to me.

That night at the prayer meeting, the living room had definitely felt sacred. The small circle of bowed heads formed its own solar system of fixed lights in the darkness. Someone would pray, softly at first and then amping up, lifted by the murmurings of solidarity from around the circle: "Yes, Lord" and "Praise You, Jesus" and a few scattered "Hallelujahs" as we prayed for our schools, for revival. The whole room hummed with holiness.

I was pretty sure the success of the thing was directly related to the vegetable oil, which is why I brought the Brummel & Brown container to the Buffalo Grove High School cafeteria that morning and why I had roped Kim and Alissa into coming with me.

The school Bible study in Mr. Stein's room was still wildly disappointing. It had been run straight into the ground by Susan and *Hell's Bells,* so the three of us had decided to take matters into our own hands. We'd recently started a prayer group, which would meet every morning in the cafeteria before school started. An alternate (superior) option for the spiritually hungry student at BG.

"All right, you guys ready?" I asked. Kim and Alissa nodded.

We dipped our fingers into the container with a manufactured solemnity. The oil felt slick, and when I lifted my fingers out, they looked greasy in the cafeteria light.

Alissa immediately got some on her shirt. "Crap," she said under her breath.

I stood, my fingers dripping as I touched the edges of the table, wanting so much to leave my mark on that school.

"God, we just pray for revival," I started, and I loved the way the word sounded on my lips—light and weighty all at once. I loved the way it looked in my imagination, the way I always felt as if we were right on the brink of it.

I pressed the oil to the table. "Lord, we claim this school for You." I believed that my words were a flag planted in the concrete. A promise taken by force of faith.

"We pray that You would grow this prayer group. That it would get too big to be contained by this cafeteria."

"Yes, Lord."

"We pray that You would take over our school."

"Amen, amen." My friends echoed, and we smiled at one another, our fingers glistening under the fluorescent lights.

At fourteen, we believed in these things. Bigness. Numbers. *Revival.* We wanted a hundred people, a thousand people, a million different voices all saying the same thing. We were freshmen, always aware of our smallness, filled to the top with vague, shimmery dreams. We wanted everything.

It would take us years to learn that this was enough: the three of us, our friendship reaching deep. That this was what we would come back to every time when it all fell apart.

five

Three-Minute Testimony: The short, polished account of one's conversion to Christianity. It covers only the highlights of one's faith story so that it can be memorized quickly, delivered simply, and pulled out at a moment's notice.

By the time the Teen Mania Summer Mission Trip Guide comes in the mail, you are stone-sunk in love with Chris. You will follow him to the end of the earth, even if he doesn't ask you to.

The guide arrives, and it fills you with both fear and excitement. You call him immediately. "How do I know which country God wants me to go to?" you ask him.

"Here's what you do," he says, his voice on the phone electric with faith. "Kneel on the floor. Draw a circle around yourself and pray. Whatever you do, don't move from that circle until God gives you an answer."

As soon as you hang up, you choose a rough patch of carpet on your basement bedroom floor. You spread the glossy brochure in front of you and kneel. You pore over every country description, every page, while a worship CD plays on repeat in the background.

You read the statistics and look at the map and wait for God to give you a heart for *one particular place.*

You wait. You wait. You wait.

You decide to limit your search to only the page with two-week mission trips (instead of Teen Mania's more typical one-month commitment). Your parents are a little unsure about this whole thing, and you seriously doubt your ability to convince them to let you go for a month. Your eyes dart between the three options: *Haiti. The Dominican Republic. Trinidad and Tobago.* You sit and you pray. You say, *Show me Your will,* and as you wait, your knees burn and your feet go numb.

You wait.

You wait.

You wait until it's clear that no voice will be coming from the heavens to give you an Answer. So instead, you close your eyes and move your finger in a circle on the page. You go around and around until you feel as if you should stop. Then you open your eyes to see where God has led you.

And that's how you end up on the Teen Mania Dominican Republic Missions Team for the summer of 1998.

— —

The Teen Mania welcome letter comes a few weeks later with its packing lists and devotional guides, including a Field Guide that you read cover to cover. You learn about how to craft a perfect three-minute testimony. *A carefully prepared testimony, empowered by the Holy Spirit, can be of immediate and effective use in nearly every witnessing situation,* it says. Like an infomercial for God. Like evangelical direct-response marketing. Jesus as a sort of Proactiv Solution for your soul.

If it were possible to take a "Before" picture of your soul, you can only imagine how it would look: red and pockmarked like the acne-riddled face. Or maybe like a plate shattered, the pieces lying in a great, sharp heap. But of course, it's not that easy. Your soul is unseeable, an immaterial essence, the part of you that lives on still when your lungs stop breathing and your heart stops beating and your eyes become fixed in your head.

If it were possible to take an "After" picture, your soul would be pink and healthy, swirling easily around your body. Before Jesus. After Jesus. Just a few easy steps to total spiritual freedom.

You've written out your testimony a dozen times before. You know that an Opportunity could arise at any moment; a testimony is the kind of thing you must always have with you, tucked invisibly in your purse next to your wallet and your pen. That way, if you have to share your faith journey with the new freshmen at youth group, you're ready. Or if someone says, "I'm just feeling so lost," you explain, in three minutes or less, how to get found. The words will be there, waiting for you, carbon copied onto your brain from all of the times you've written and rewritten them on paper.

It's not hard to write it out. At age fourteen, you have a story so straightforward, so simple to tell. Follow a three-point outline, the guide says. "My life with Christ." (Emphasize point "c" below if you became a Christian as a small child.)

a. *Life BEFORE knowing Christ.* You were, of course, only a child. But you were a sinner. You once stole a handful of root beer barrels out of the candy jar at Roy and Hilda's house next door. When your mom walked into your bedroom and found you counting your loot, she marched you straight over there, and between the humiliation of it and the guilt of it, you couldn't stop crying. You could barely get the words out to ask forgiveness.

b. *HOW you came to know Christ (be specific):* You asked Jesus into your heart. Said the Sinner's Prayer after that terrible dream about hell. You write the words like a template for salvation: *Dear Jesus, I believe that You died for my sins and rose from the dead. I pray that You would forgive me of my sins and that You would come into my heart and make me new. In Your name I pray, Amen.* It's good to give an example like this when you tell people your testimony. That way, they know how to do it later on, lying in their beds at home. If they are moved while they are thinking about the day, thinking about your testimony, thinking about their pockmarked souls.

c. *Life AFTER you received Christ (changes He has made—*
what He means to you now). Of course, for you, most of
your life has been After. And even the Before part was
saturated with God. It's not as though you didn't believe
and then you did. You were always growing toward
belief, until one day you "said the prayer" that made you
new. But that kind of logic isn't going to convince anyone
to become a Christian. People want to believe in a visible
kind of change. Something they can experience. A
magnified Before and After, which look distinctly
different. So you say, "Now that Christ is in my life, I
have purpose and I have a Friend who will never leave
me. I know that I will never have to be lonely again." You
don't realize that you are lying to them, at least about the
lonely part. You don't realize that you're lying to yourself.

1. *Begin with an interesting, attention-getting sentence and close*
with a good conclusion.

     ~~Hi. My name is Addie…~~

     ~~Have you ever experienced the fires of hell? Well, I did~~
~~once. Of course, it was only in a nightmare…~~

     ~~If you died tonight, are you 100 percent sure that you~~
~~would go to heaven?…~~

     Hi. My name is Addie.

2. *Don't use Christianese words such as "saved," "convicted,"*
"converted," "born again," and "sin." They do not communicate
truth to the average non-Christian. Though these words and
phrases are precious to us, they are so often misunderstood and
consequently ridiculed by non-Christians.

     Saved. Recovered. Rescued. Salvaged. Bailed out. Revived.
Resuscitated.

     ~~I was dying and Jesus resuscitated me…~~

~~I was in the prison of my sin and Jesus bailed me out.~~

Jesus rescued me from my ~~sin~~ wrongdoings, and now I am His. ~~I've been born again.~~ I have a new life, and when I die, I know I'll go to heaven.

3. *Smile often! Ask the Lord to give you a happy, radiant face.* You practice in your mirror, trying to look up from your note cards frequently and send an easy grin into the reflective glass. *Hi. My name is Addie.* Your two front teeth overlap a little bit; the dentist says you're going to have to have braces, but you keep begging your mom to wait because you hate the thought of having a mouthful of metal. Now, as you stand there, reading your faith into the mirror, you are superaware of the imperfections of your face, your mouth, your teeth, your awful *crooked* teeth, and no one is going to pay any attention to you when you look like this. You sigh. Start again. *Hi. My name is Addie…*

4. *Practice your testimony until it becomes natural.* But of course, it never does, because it is a completely unnatural medium of communication. Even at fourteen, you can't sum up your entire journey in three minutes, one hundred and eighty seconds.

Tick, tick, tick.

Before. After.

Trapped. Free. Dirty. Clean. Sad. Happy.

A perfect dichotomy.

Tick, tick, tick.

In the Before picture, your soul is shattered, the pieces lying in a great, sharp heap. After, it is pink and healthy. The three-minute testimony is not about the in between. About the other millions of seconds that define your life, the seconds during which your soul will shatter again and again and again. Break and heal and break and heal, an endless circle of pain and restoration that is life.

"Hi. My name is Addie. I used to be lost; now I am found."

[Look up. Smile at the small crowd before you. Ask the Lord to give you a happy, radiant face.]

"What happened to me was this…"

Tick, tick, tick, tick.

Six

Short-Term Mission Trip: A person or team is sent to spread the Good News in a country or region in which evangelical faith is not widely practiced. This is a popular activity for youth groups, exposing students to the needs of the world while teaching them to bravely share their faith.

Hold still," Bridget said. She was bent over my face, a glob of white paint gleaming on her poised finger. I planted my hands on my knees, stiffening at the feel of the cold, thick paste against my cheek as she began to spread the makeup over my skin.

It was July, two weeks after Chris had finally said *I love you,* three weeks before he would leave for Texas for his yearlong Teen Mania internship. It was the summer of my first love. I marked time by his coming and going.

I was sitting on top of a picnic table under the great thatched shelter that comprised the center of the Teen Mania Missionary Base in the Dominican Republic. Each morning and evening we met there for meals. At night, we gathered for worship, our tired bodies leaning against the hard ledges of the picnic tables while the sky grew dark around us.

That morning, sun streaked through the flowering trees and across the grass. It fell onto the laps and backs and hands of the rest of the Teen Mania Missionary Teams as they moved in the rhythms of morning preparation. Soon, each team would board its own balmy yellow bus. The buses would vibrate with zydeco music as they carried us all to separate, tucked-under places of the Dominican countryside so that we could perform a drama.

The drama was the same one Chris had done in Australia, and I felt linked to him by the choreography and the music, the same story narrated in Spanish above me.

The drama was about a Good Captain and an Evil Pirate King... but not really. *Really* it was about Jesus and Satan and their battle for the allegiance of the shipmates. *Really* it was about the Cross and the Resurrection and the altar call at the end, where one of us would stand and give our three-minute testimony. It was about yellow index cards that were distributed to the audience so that Teen Mania could keep track of how many souls it had saved in the Dominican Republic that week.

Bridget spread the white makeup around the outline of my face. My freshly cut blond hair was tied back, and when she finished, my skin would be a wall of white.

My role in the drama was a mime; not part of the story but rather its backdrop. I was a piece of a portable stage: a plank of the ship, then a rock on the island shore. My feet tingled sharply as I listened several times a day to wooden swords clashing during the dramatic climax. The dust stung my open eyes, and the gravel pressed into my knees, yet I remained perfectly still.

—— —

I had been late getting out of the cabin that morning. Bridget was not happy. She'd already washed her hands when I approached her timidly, begging her to help me apply my mime makeup.

I didn't have the courage to tell her I was late because I defied the two-minute shower limit so I could shave my legs.

Teen Mania Ministries structured its mission trips in a way that made it difficult to fall into the shallows of vanity. Twelve girls shared a single small dorm room. Twelve teen girls and two showers. A tall girl named Nicole enforced two-minute shower limits by shouting over the sound of falling water, "One minute left!" then "Thirty seconds!"

It was a premeditated act of vanity, this shaving. I snuck the razor with me into the shower, thinking that I could somehow manage to squeeze it all in during my two minutes. But I went over my time allotment by almost sixty seconds.

When I emerged from the shower, Nicole was glaring at me. I mumbled an apology and grabbed a wad of toilet paper to blot the tiny cuts beading along my razor-burned legs. There were girls on our team who had given up on shaving for the trip, letting the hair on their legs grow long and fine. But I couldn't do it. I needed the legs under my black scrubs to feel like my own, even as I knelt on the dusty road and became a rock.

I grabbed a palette of face paint from one of the picnic tables and held it up in front of Bridget. She was smoothing the hair under her red pirate bandana. "Please?"

She looked me up and down and sighed. "Fine," she said. "Sit down."

—◆—

Here is how you become a mime: you flub your drama audition at Teen Mania headquarters in Garden Valley, Texas. On the day you arrive, you are herded onto the tennis courts with a group of people you do not yet know, and you are told to mimic the choreographed movements of the blond woman up front.

The music starts loudly, unexpectedly, blaring over speakers at the edges of the tennis courts, and you are terrible at dancing. You have always known this about yourself, and you know it all the more as you crash into the tall Texan on your right while trying to imitate something that looks like a grapevine. Your arms smack haphazardly into the dancers on either side of you, who try to ignore your erratic movements. You see your team leader look at you and make a broad stroke on his clipboard. And you know.

Or maybe you become a mime before that. Maybe it starts in a great convention hall back in November, when you attend Teen Mania's Acquire The Fire conference. You do not know the true meaning of "Mania" then—"excessive, unreasonable enthusiasm," a word commonly associated with bipolar disorder. You know only that your heart is beating loud and that Chris is sitting beside you, his pen suspended over his official conference program.

The director of Teen Mania is pacing the stage, talking about the countercultural revolution that began in the sixties: a revolt against conservative, godly values. His face is magnified on the screen above, his dark hair gelled so that it crests at his forehead. He speaks in italics, in the measured voice of practiced brokenness.

"If you want to be part of a new movement, come forward now," he says. "If you want to go overseas this summer, the summer of 1998, and spread the gospel to a generation in great turmoil…don't stay in your seat. Don't look at the person next to you. Just come."

But you do look at the person next to you, because the person next to you is Chris, and you are completely in love with him.

In the corner of your eye, you see the great room shifting, hundreds of teenagers streaming down stairwells, down concrete steps to the crowded floor below. Chris stands. You stand. You move forward as if you are attached to him by an invisible thread. When you look at him, and when you look at the director on stage, you are in awe. You are convinced that their eyes are filled with the light of God. It does not occur to you that the light you think you see is crazed, unrestrained obsession, wild as wind.

You are fourteen. You have not learned to weigh words for truth or let logic penetrate emotion. You know only the warmth of Chris's body next to your own, the mix of his Aspen cologne with the fervent, sweaty words of the speaker. You *want* mania. Even if you could understand its definition, its sinister undertones, you still might want it. When you are fourteen, truth matters less than the sound of your own heart pumping in your ears, the excitement of being swept up into something greater than yourself.

— · —

Bridget finished my left cheek and bent down to get another dollop of face paint. I watched, my face still as stone, as her finger arched up over my eyebrows. She was the female pirate in the drama. Her left cheek sported a stylish black scar, her right cheek, a white skull and crossbones. She wore a flowy black skirt with a rope around her waist. Like the other shipmates, her face was distinctive, colorful. Beautiful. I envied her desperately.

I took a deep breath. I could still smell the remains of breakfast on the air. The morning before, at that very table, I'd tried to hide a hard-boiled egg in a napkin.

Teen Mania had a Rule about eating everything placed in front of you, and I wanted to be the kind of person who could muster up mind over matter and eat a hard-boiled egg like a grownup. But in the end, I couldn't do it. I looked around to see if anyone was watching, and then I tucked it into the napkin on my lap. Casually, I placed the napkin on my plate, as though it was nothing but paper.

Christina was the one who caught me. Before I could stop her, she began scooping up trash. She was wearing her Arabian Knight costume—a plastic sword looped into the side of her airy pants. As soon as she touched it, the napkin fell open to reveal my egg: round, white, untouched.

"Whose egg is this?" Christina asked, looking pointedly around the table. Everyone was silent, looking sideways at one another. I did not claim the egg, but their gazes landed heavily on me as I moved my shaking hands to clear away the napkin.

"What if one of the cooks sees this egg in the garbage and is offended?" she said to no one in particular.

She sat down, abandoning her cleaning. "What if she thinks Christians are wasteful and ungrateful people?

"What if she goes to hell?"

She was giving me an opening to offer my confession. I could have apologized. I could have taken the egg out of the napkin and eaten it as penance.

But I didn't. I finished collecting the paper plates and napkins on the table. I picked up the uneaten egg and walked to the garbage can, and I had the distinct feeling that they were watching me go.

Chris would have been disappointed if he'd known about that egg. He'd tried to prepare me for all of this. One rainy spring day, he and his Teen Mania friend Drew (in town for a long weekend) took me to a gazebo for lunch. I thought we were just having a picnic.

I lifted a peanut butter and jelly sandwich out of my paper sack. "Don't *let* me hear you complain about this food!" screamed Drew, this boy I barely knew. The sudden angry burst made me look up, shocked.

Drew looked at his watch and sighed. "You're wasting time. You have two more minutes to finish eating, and then you are going out there in the rain to do the drama."

"What drama?" I asked. "What are you talking about?" I looked at Chris for an explanation. He gave me a little wink. His dimple flashed almost imperceptibly across his cheek, and I grinned.

"Ahh!! Sunflower!" Drew shouted, pointing at me accusingly with his entire arm, his entire body. Chris looked at me, the smile gone.

"Okay," I said, throwing down my sandwich on the bench next to me. *"What?"*

They exchanged looks. "This is missionary training," Chris said finally, with a triumphant grin.

"We're preparing you for your summer Teen Mania trip." Drew took a bite of his sandwich and then waved it at me. "See this PB&J? This is all you're going to be getting for two weeks, so you'd better learn to enjoy it." I looked at him wide-eyed, and I hated him a little bit—this fat stranger who was ruining our perfectly romantic picnic with all this talk of PB&J. Outside the gazebo, the rain was falling, falling, and I wanted to be running through it, laughing wildly. I just wanted to be in love.

"You have to eat whatever they serve you," Chris clarified. "And rain or shine, you're going to be performing that drama."

"Ahh," I said, the pieces beginning to click in place. "And the sunflower thing?"

"That," said Chris, "is the most important part."

"Sunflowers follow the sun," Drew explained, his mouth still full of sandwich. "When it's dark out, they face downward. But when the sun comes out, they follow its course across the sky." He made a long, slow arch with his finger.

"At Teen Mania, a sunflower is a girl who's into a guy. And when he's not there, she's like, sad. But then he comes into a room, and she lights up. Got it?"

I understood that this was bad. I knew from the Acquire The Fire conference and from the Summer Missions pamphlet that there would be no dating allowed at Teen Mania, that you were supposed to go on your mission with a single focus: reaching the lost for the Lord. Attraction, love, dating: these things had no place in the world of Teen Mania. I nodded mechanically, painfully aware of my face. "Okay," I said. "I won't be a sunflower."

"Good," said Chris. "Then your training is complete."

—•—

"Turn your head," Bridget said, squirting more face paint onto her finger. I turned to the left, and my thoughts drifted to the girl I did not know. The one who was sent home just the other night.

She had broken one of Teen Mania's Rules for girl-boy conduct, which were complex and unforgiving. (No holding hands, no hugs, no

sitting together on the school bus. Anything smacking of romantic en-
tanglement—*Sunflower!*—became grounds for immediate dismissal.
"Bon Voyage," they called it, "BV" for short.)

Rumor was she went out alone on a kayak with a Dominican transla-
tor during a free day at the beach. And then, she was gone. No good-byes,
no explanations…just an empty cot where her sleeping bag used to be. I
didn't know what her name was, and no one would say it. They regarded
her in the hushed whisper that people use when speaking of the dead.

This will all unravel for you in a few years. Some well-meaning person
will describe the Holy Trinity as an egg: the shell, the white, and the yolk
all distinct, yet part of the same entity. Or you will be boiling eggs for
Easter. You will be watching them float in the water, the pressure and the
heat reforming them into that strange new solid. And you will realize that
you are just so *angry*. You will wonder why everything has to be about
something else. You will wonder why an egg can't just be an egg, or why
a sunflower can't just be a sunflower…why a girl can't just be a girl.

You will get so irritated that you will lose track of how long the eggs
have been boiling. When it finally occurs to you to take them out, you
will notice a network of tiny fractures perforating their delicate white
shells.

"Almost done," Bridget said. "Close your eyes now." I waited for the familiar stroke of the black eyeliner. I could feel the paint cross my eyebrows, my eyelids, the puffy ridges underneath my eyes. These lines were
the worst part. When Bridget pulled the eyeliner sharply over my eyes, I
felt as though I were being crossed out.

What I wanted most of all was for Chris to appear from the bunch
of palm trees ahead of me. I wanted to ask him if this was *really* what it
was supposed to feel like—the missionary life.

I wanted to tell him about the little old woman with chronic head-aches at our drama site the other day, small and frail in a raggedy dress. I wanted to tell him how we crowded in on her and her husband to invoke the name of Jesus Christ. I'd held her hand; it felt tiny in my palm.

We prayed as Teen Mania taught us: repetitive words with a kind of lyric pacing. After the prayer was finished, everyone looked up expectantly. They told us during training that our prayers were like weapons, that if we believed strongly enough, there would be miracles. We would *see* God move.

"How do you feel?" someone asked tentatively.

The woman smiled, hugged us all. She did not comment on her headache, but her smile seemed proof enough for the group. Later, when we returned to our base, the team spun it as a story of a miraculous healing.

But I was haunted by her smile, her touch, her scrap-metal house in the shantytown by the mountain, where structures leaned precariously into each other. I was troubled by the glimmer of glass in the streets, the children barefoot upon it. I wanted Chris to *explain* this to me. I wanted him to make me believe that she was really cured the way the others believed it. I wanted to know that all this was worth it.

"Close your *eyes*!" Bridget said again. I obeyed, and I could see the scene as if I was right there: the woman standing behind our bus with her husband, waving. Children clung to the back of the bus and ran alongside the windows as we drove away.

———

One day you will learn the words *thought reform,* a term coined by re-nowned American psychiatrist Robert Lifton to describe what was happening to POWs during the Korean War, to the students in Communist China under Mao.

Reform. It is a positive word, indicating a subtle betterment of the self. A term for which Merriam-Webster has nothing but praise: "to put or change into an improved form or condition." Or "to abandon evil ways." *She used to shave her legs, run her fingers along her hair while talking to a boy. She used to light up like a sunflower when he came into a room. But she has been reformed. Synonyms: See* CORRECT.

Only in its most scientific definition does the word *reform* reveal anything of its violent nature. To subject to cracking. To produce by cracking. *Cracking.* An incomplete brokenness. Fracture. Split. Splinter. Snap. Almost imperceptible at first, these fissures along the skin, but they leave you exposed, delicate. One blow, and you will crumble into dust.

It's not, of course, the perfect term. *Reform* suggests that you have already been solidified into a self. You were not. You were barely fifteen. You learn that the brain is not fully formed until you're twenty-five years old, and you wonder, then, what becomes of the mind commandeered before it has learned to follow paths of logic.

You were soft as clay straight from the earth. You were reformed before you were formed.

— —

"Okay," Bridget said, wiping the residual white paint off her hands with a brown paper napkin. "You're done. Just wait for it to dry."

"Thanks," I said, but she was already gone.

I lay back on the picnic table and looked up at the thatched roof, at the streams of light shining through the gaps. I could feel the places on my face where the paint was still liquid, fluid—where it had yet to harden into disguise.

"God predestined you to be a mime," our team leader had said on the day roles were assigned. I closed my eyes and wondered if maybe I was a mime not so much because of God but because of me. Because I couldn't seem to leave my legs unshaven or swallow a hard-boiled egg. I was out of step. Out of time.

A shadow passed overhead and stopped. I slit open my eyes, and there, standing above me, was a boy. A mime. His face was chalky, eyes bisected with dark, straight lines.

I recognized him immediately.

We had met on our free day. We had spent the morning among Dominican vendors selling wooden toys and wrap skirts and shot glasses and had returned early to two separate buses parked next to each other. We were sitting on the sticky canvas seats, waiting for things to move.

He looked out his window at me. I looked out my window at him.

We smiled like sunflowers.

It was enough to get us in serious trouble, but the buses were hot and empty. There had been the festive air of the bazaar, the loud voices of the vendors, the ocean breeze on my skin—and it had made me forget for a second that I was a Teen Mania missionary.

Instead, I was just a girl, looking at a boy through a window.

The boy smiled. *Open your window,* he mouthed. And, with a quick glance around to make sure no one was watching, I did.

"What's your name?"

"Addie. What's yours?"

"Justin." He reached a hand across the space between our two buses.

A handshake.

A *long* handshake.

Practically a handhold.

A ticket home if anyone were to see us *(Bon Voyage!)*. But there, in the space between the buses, I held on to his hand and smiled, and he held on to mine and smiled back.

American voices began to approach, the shuffling of plastic bags. "Here," he said suddenly. He used his free hand to push a brown beaded bracelet from his wrist to mine. "Something to remember me by." The bracelet snapped into place over my small wrist, and suddenly, we were both laughing—a sort of morbid hilarity. It was the illicit pleasure of touch, one hand holding another in the Dominican heat, in the face of

rules that barred such innocent things, like a boy meeting a girl and saying hello.

— —

At the picnic table, I finally found my voice enough to say a hoarse,
"Hey." I shielded my eyes with my hand so I could see him better. The
paint on our faces matched so precisely that it was almost like looking in
a mirror.

Justin grinned. Then he looked quickly around. When he decided
the coast was clear, he looked slyly down at me. And winked. And then
he was gone.

I lay there for a moment, and then, for no particular reason, I began
to laugh.

The white paint on my face cracked in a thousand places.

Underneath, there was skin—my face, breaking through, touching
the light.

Seven

Jesus Freak: A phrase coined in the late sixties to refer
(derogatively) to those involved in the Jesus Movement. It
was revived and reclaimed in the evangelical culture in the
late nineties when leading Christian rock band DC Talk
released its popular album *Jesus Freak,* inviting Christians
everywhere to let their freak-flags fly and embrace their
unique identity.

Did you *see* those guys?" Alissa whispered as we walked into the
building.

I nodded wordlessly. So did Kim on the other side of me. We had, of
course, seen the guys out front. They were hard to miss, spiked through
as they were with all manner of jewelry, sharp metal glittering menac-
ingly from all over their faces. They were casually leaning against the
sloped roof that angled sharply to the ground, giving the building itself
the look of a giant triangle. They were taking long drags from their cigarettes and watching us coolly as we passed by in typical suburban teen
summer garb: jean shorts and T-shirts, flip-flops clopping rhythmically
as we shuffled in through the door.

The place was called Vertical Impact, and if you had to assign it a
descriptive phrase, it would be *youth church.* Every Saturday, teenagers
from the far reaches of the northwest suburbs of Chicago trickled inside
to the thumping of the drumbeat and the amped-up sound of passion-
filled, high-mobility worship. The back of the building had been turned

into a trendy coffee bar with graffiti-covered booths and a cappuccino machine.

Vertical Impact was meant to have edges, teeth. It was meant for guys like the ones outside with their spiky jewelry and bad attitudes. I liked how different the graffitied dark of this church felt from Deerbrook, with its sunlit corridors and smiling greeters, who smelled of peppermint and potpourri.

I liked the "come as you are" sort of feel. I liked that, once you were in the door, you were sucked into a kind of undertow, an inescapable pull toward God and Jesus and all manner of Revival.

Alissa, Kim, and I did not have tattoos or nose piercings. We were clearly not the intended audience of Vertical Impact. But we were welcomed anyway, especially tonight, when the place had become a concert venue for the popular Christian ska band, the Insyderz. We paid for our tickets at the door, one by one handing folded dollar bills to a kid with blue hair, one by one entering the fray.

We stood there, side by side, pushed against the wall of the building by the movement of kids pressing in.

"Chris has to be around here somewhere," I said, peering into the crowd, looking for a bald head bobbing around. It was Chris, of course, who'd first brought me here a few months ago. I'd tagged behind him as he'd given fist pumps and high-fives to tall guys with full sleeves of tattoos. More than once that night, he'd forgotten that I was there, a quiet shadow hovering behind him, and stepped on me as he turned to say hello to someone else.

"This is insane," Kim said, looking across the crowded room.

"I feel like I should have worn a different outfit." Alissa glanced at her knobby, freshman-almost-sophomore knees and then out at the sea of baggy jeans and metal belts.

"We just need to get some coffee," I said with manufactured confidence. "We'll look more at home if we have something in our hands."

Kim tugged at her Old Navy T-shirt, and we weaved single-file through the crowd. And then he was there, next to us suddenly, leaning against the coffee counter. "You guys made it!" he said, smiling at me hugely.

"We did!" I said. He wore a white T-shirt and his skin was deeply tanned. In a few days he would leave for Texas, but now he was here, and *I* was here, and not even the scary punk-rock guys out front could ruin this moment for me.

Alissa and Kim sidled up next to me with their drinks. "Hey, guys," Chris said casually, giving them a little nod.

"Hey," they mumbled in tandem. They didn't know Chris very well. Since he didn't go to our high school and Kim and Alissa only occasionally visited my church youth group, they'd seen him in real life just a couple of times. They knew him mostly by my gushy descriptions and by my long jag of sobbing during our nonbreakup breakup a few months earlier. I looked at them next to me and grinned wide. Alissa was clearly trying not to stare at his freshly reshaved head.

"Well, I have to go talk to some people, but you guys should hurry up and finish your coffee. These guys rock, and you're gonna want to be out there in the middle of everything when they start."

"Yeah," I said quickly. "That's what we were thinking," even though we were decidedly *not* thinking that.

"Cool," he said, tipping his head back. "I'll catch up with you gals later."

At an empty table, we set down our coffee and Kim's voice went super high-pitched as she crooned, "He's so dreeeeamy!" and Alissa laughed. I stuck my tongue out at them and sipped my cappuccino.

"But seriously," Kim said. "When does he leave for Texas?"

"Tuesday," I sighed.

"That sucks." Alissa blew the steam from over her giant coffee mug.

"It's God's will…" I trailed off, distracted by a group of very punk-rock-looking girls who had taken over the table next to us. They wore their hair short and spiky. They rocked ultraflared pants and tight thrift-store tops, and the rings in their noses seemed to belong there. They were Christians and thus somewhat alienated from normal high school culture, but they *pulled it off*. It was as though they couldn't care less what anyone thought. Their purses were made of duct tape. They wore giant, spike-studded belts. I looked at them for a long moment, and I coveted their coolness.

"You guys are going to stay together, though, right?" Alissa asked.

"Of course!" I realized that I'd said it kind of loud and lowered my voice. "I mean, he's doing it for God, you know? And what kind of girlfriend would I be if I just broke up with him because he was following God's plan?"

Kim and Alissa nodded and sipped. The coffee was almost all sugar, but we pretended it was the real thing, that we were adult enough to be drinking it, adult enough to have conversations about long-distance relationships and unending love.

The room filled all at once with screams, and we craned our necks to see the Insyderz appearing on stage. The music began, and they were mixing trombone and guitar and drums and piano, performing a crazed, punk-rock version of the well-known worship song "Awesome God."

The Insyderz was just one of the new bands on the Christian music scene. The members too were tattooed and pierced; they had done their best to make themselves indistinguishable from secular rock stars. They understood the lure of the anti-establishment punk-rock beat, and they had co-opted it, stretched it tight around the lyrics of God. They wanted you to know that you didn't have to listen to crappy music to be a Christian. They believed Christians could rock just as hard as anyone else, so they made their voices loud and rough and belted it out again, "Our God is an AWESOME GOD!"

"We should go up there!" I yelled. Kim nodded.

Alissa's eyes went wide, but she screamed, "Okay!" We left our mugs on the table and worked our way toward the stage. The lead singer's voice was rough and loud along the familiar lyrics, and everyone around us was jumping up and down.

"What do we do?" Alissa yelled.

"Jump, I guess!" And so we did, our flip-flops smacking unforgivingly as we came down hard on the carpet.

We didn't realize until too late that the jumping was getting a little moshy, that the moshiness was turning into a riptide, that Alissa was being sucked into the mess of people. We lost her in the sea of unnaturally black hair and ripped T-shirts and spiked necklaces.

"Where did she go?" I shouted.

"I don't know!" Kim stood on her toes, looking for Alissa's brown hair.

"She's in flip-flops!"

"Stay here," Kim said, not taking her eyes off the throbbing group of teens. "I'm going in."

She elbowed her way into the group, jabbing hard and purposefully into the sides of strangers until they let her through. She disappeared into the middle as into a swirling vortex. On stage, the cheeks of the trombone player were turning red. He was rocking his instrument back and forth, his high tops purposefully untied on both feet. The lead singer was already sweating under the fluorescent lights.

My gaze darted back from the stage to the mosh pit when Kim came out, triumphant, her hand locked around Alissa's. Alissa's brown hair was electric with static and she was limping a little. "We're getting out of here," Kim said firmly.

I nodded and cast one last look around the room. I couldn't see Chris, and I felt my loyalty split between my friends and the boy. But he was nowhere. I reluctantly turned and followed Kim and Alissa through the door and out into the night.

The guys out front were still leaning, statuesque, against the walls, smoke spiraling from their cigarette stubs as they looked at the sky. We walked past them to the edge of the building and sat down on the side-walk. Alissa took deep breaths and tried not to cry. "I wasn't ready for that," she said.

"We're totally not going back in there." Kim looked at me for confirmation, and I nodded a little sadly. Next door, Wendy's sat lit and welcoming with familiar booths and predictable menu items. I looked at it and then looked back at the door, but Chris was not there. I wanted him to be watching over us, over *me*, to come out and make it all okay.

I let my gaze linger for a moment, but he did not come.

"Let's go to Wendy's," I said. "You need a Frosty."

Kim nodded. "And french fries."

Alissa smiled. We grabbed her by the arms and together walked away.

Eight

True Love Waits: An international campaign aimed at teenagers and college students, promoting sexual abstinence outside of marriage. Created in April 1993, True Love Waits encourages students to be faithful to their future spouses by refraining from all acts of sexual impurity, including watching pornography and giving in to lust.

Your church holds a True Love Waits banquet toward the end of your freshman year of high school. The movement is only four years old, still trendy and gaining momentum in evangelical youth culture. Your parents attend, your mom chatting idly with another couple at the table, your dad shifting quietly in his seat, rubbing his graying beard, somewhat uncomfortable with all of this talk about sex.

The lights dim. The youth pastor speaks. Then a skit:

A girl stands on stage alone. Around her neck hangs a red paper heart.

She is deeply and perfectly happy. You can tell by the way she dances around the invisible boundaries of the stage, holding her red heart out to admire it and then clasping it to her chest in a sort of embrace.

The heart is perfectly symmetrical, bright red like a Valentine. It is inaccurate in its perfection, a simplistic rendering of the real human heart with its chambers and valves, arteries and veins. It's symbolic, of course—but it is this false heart that you envision in your own chest, pumping soft and red behind your ribs.

Back on stage, the girl is trying to share her red heart. She tries her parents first, but they are distracted and irritated and end up ripping a piece away, leaving the heart mangled around the girl's neck. There are no words, just a Jars of Clay CD playing in the background, soft lyrics about falling in love with Jesus.

A group of teens stroll across the stage, and the girl hands them her heart, happy to be in their company. But before long, they have gone, ripping away another chunk of red and taking it with them. Then, of course, there is the boyfriend. He is the worst of all. He rips a large chunk of paper right from the center of the distorted paper heart and stomps on it. *Stomps on it!*

The girl is fake crying. She is picking the pieces of her heart off the ground and holding them to her chest, as if trying to reassemble herself.

Enter Chris. He is dressed in a white shirt, dressed to represent Jesus in this skit.

You sit up a little straighter.

Chris takes the broken heart from around the girl's neck and puts it around his own. He pantomimes an agonizing death on an imaginary cross and then rises out of it to give the girl a new heart. White. Pure. Unbroken.

The girl is deeply and perfectly happy. It is as if none of the ripping ever happened. She embraces Jesus. Chris. You feel a twinge of jealousy.

You look down at the wallet-sized pledge card on the table before you. *Believing that true love waits, I make a commitment to God, myself, my family, my friends, my future mate, and my future children to be sexually abstinent from this day until the day I enter a biblical marriage relationship.* You think about the ripped heart, and you think you can prevent it by signing this card, so you do. Your signature is small, loopy, unpracticed.

You think of this phrase, this movement, *True Love Waits,* a lot toward the end of that summer. Chris is packing his bags with Teen Mania–approved clothing. He is getting ready for his year as an intern at their headquarters in Texas. You spend your summer days helping him shop for things that he will need in his dorm away from home. Sheets.

Shampoo. Extension cords. At night, you go on long walks together under the warm, dark sky.

One night, you walk across the street from Chris's house to an elementary school. Everything is still. The moon is shining bright over the slides, and the whole playground is glowing around you. You stop at a big map of the United States painted on the blacktop, careful lines dissecting the sprawling country into all of its various states.

You smile and grab Chris's hand. You pull him to the big, outlined shape of Texas. Then you move to stand in Illinois and assess the space between you.

"See?" you say. "It's not that far." If you both were to reach out your arms, your fingers would almost brush up against one another.

He smiles but says nothing as he stands in Texas, looking up at the moon. From your space in Illinois, you can still see the smooth surface of his shaved head. You can see the outlines of his muscles as he plunges his hands into his pockets. You can almost see the thoughts whirring around in his head.

There is no question in your mind that you will wait for him, that you will be here in the Midwest, staring intently down toward Texas. When he gets back a year from now, he will find you just as he left you, arms open wide.

He doesn't ask you to wait. But he doesn't tell you not to either, and you are fifteen. You are in love for the first time, and you know that True Love Waits. It's only a year, after all. What else are you going to do?

— • —

It is the end of summer and Chris is gone, but you are doing just fine. In fact, you are away. You are with your youth group, visiting your church's previous youth pastor at his new home in Michigan. You are on a boat in the middle of the lake, the silence billowing softly around you.

You lean your head back. The sky is clear, and you are aware of the enormity of the universe above, around, in you. And you know: *God is here.* He is all around. He fills completely the void between earth and heaven. The wind stirs, and it feels like a whisper.

Someone begins to sing a worship song, and you are surprised by the sound of your own voice joining in, its hopeful warble blending into the night. "You're all I want," the song says, and in this moment, you completely believe it, though your heart feels cavernous in its emptiness, and you ache for Chris's hand.

Everyone is singing now, and it is spontaneous, unplanned, a necessary response to the holiness you feel in the air. You sing, one song ending, someone starting another, worship strung together like lights on a string until the last song ends, and the sound of that final note is so perfect, so absolute, that you all somehow know it is time to turn the motor back on, go back in.

It seems impossible to go inside that night, so all the girls sleep on the big backyard trampoline, bare feet in the middle, heads at the edges like the spangles of a star. You lie on the black vinyl, small beneath the far-reaching sky, but held. You feel absolutely secure, absolutely loved, wrapped in the great mystery of God's love. And for the time being, it almost doesn't matter that Chris is a thousand miles away. You are in love with Jesus. It is almost entirely enough.

—▪ —

Sophomore year begins and you take your required health class with Mrs. Roth. You are unprepared for the sex education piece of it, and you could almost die from discomfort on the day she passes around a model of the female anatomy and a plastic diaphragm.

Today's classroom activity: practice squeezing the diaphragm into an oval and inserting it into the plastic vagina so that it rests snugly against the plastic pubic bone. When the uterus comes your way, you try to pass it quickly to the kid in front of you, but Mrs. Roth catches you.

"Young lady," she says, "I didn't see you practice."

You shift uncomfortably in your seat. "I don't plan on having sex until I'm married," you say.

In the classroom around you, you hear people shift in their seats, a few snickers, a couple of outright laughs. Mrs. Roth eyes you. She is tiny and ruthless, her short hair coiffed over bemused eyes.

You feel your cheeks redden as you hold the giant plastic uterus in one hand and the small latex dome in the other. You close your eyes briefly and try to think of Jesus. You hope that later someone will ask you why you've chosen abstinence, and you can tell them about the mangled heart and the new, pure, unbroken one that Christ offers.

"Well," she says finally, "that may be what you think now, but abstinence is not a realistic option for most people. So you *will* practice with the diaphragm so that when you change your mind, you'll be prepared."

"But I'm not going to—," you begin to protest.

"Now."

The entire class turns to look at you. Mrs. Roth folds her arms across her small chest.

Your hands are shaking as you clumsily fold the diaphragm and jam it into the plastic opening. You have worked so hard, so diligently, to distance yourself from all of this. At night, when other teenagers are tracing the curves of their bodies with their own fingers, thinking about sex and love and lust, all of it lumped together in one great pulsing Need, you are reading your Bible. You are memorizing verses. You are dancing in your room to worship songs and thinking about God.

You have somehow managed to divorce love from sex in your mind, and so when you think about your future with Chris, with your husband, with any man, you don't think about flesh against flesh, about sweat and humanity and the physicality of love. You have heard enough sermons about Waiting, about abstinence, about how living in sin destroys your chances for a good marriage. You have come to believe that the worst thing you could ever do is to have sex before you are married.

In your mind, you have built a sort of retaining wall to hold out any thoughts of sex. You stay behind it while around you, your peers dive awkwardly into the physical fray. To you, love remains ethereal, like the fuzzy last kiss in a movie. All romance and innocence…and then…nothing. Just the end credits.

You feel like crying as you hold the plastic vagina, your classmates looking on with pursed lips and raised eyebrows. But you don't cry. You blink hard and look up instead. You have no idea if you're doing this right.

Mrs. Roth seems satisfied. "Now pass it along," she says. "We're wasting time."

———

In 1997, the book *I Kissed Dating Goodbye* hits the evangelical world like a bomb. On the cover of the sepia-toned book, a man pulls a brown brimmed hat from his head as though he is about to take it off. Chris lends you his copy before he leaves for Texas. "I really think you should read this," he says.

The main idea of the book is that dating is a doomed system that leads not to lifelong love, but to heartache…and worse, sexual impurity. The book advocates instead for a new/old concept: *courtship,* that careful formation of romantic attachment only when the end goal is marriage.

"I just don't know," Chris says on the phone one day. He is calling you from the pay phone in the hallway of his dorm in Texas. You can hear the muffled sounds of other guys behind him. "I don't think we should be together unless we're serious about marriage."

The word *marriage* doesn't scare you the way it maybe should. In the language of evangelical relationships, marriage is the pinnacle, the goal, a summit that you've been climbing toward. You are only a sophomore in high school when this conversation occurs, but you are certain that Chris is the man you will marry.

"I *am* serious about it," you say.

There is a pause.

"I'm going to be a missionary, you know." You hear the determination in his voice. You imagine him staring out over the red Texas dirt where just a few months ago you practiced your part as a mime for that Dominican Republic missions trip.

"I know," you say. It comes out as a whisper.

"Do you have what it takes to be a missionary wife?" he asks. "I mean, seriously? Do you think you could give birth on the floor of a hut in Africa?"

You pause. You remember the red dirt and the way it coated everything, the grimy feel of it against your skin. You remember the hot sun on your hair as you spent hours crouching down in that gospel drama.

But then you remember Chris. You think about the small gap between his two front teeth and about his blue eyes and you remember the way he looked at you that night when he said *love*. And you think maybe it's enough.

"Well, I don't know that I have what it takes *right now*," you reply sagely, "but I know I'll get there—God will get me to that point."

"Yeah," he says absently.

You are only a sophomore in high school, but in this instant, that doesn't seem to matter. You are timeless, swept into a great romance. You are on the edge of courtship, on the edge of marriage. You feel ready for all of it.

— —

When he comes home for Christmas, you are waiting for him at the airport, waiting with his mother who is staring out the window at all the snow. It is a pre-9/11 world, and you are waiting at the terminal, watching the planes cut through the white, watching men in orange windbreakers wave flags and push luggage into the heavy winter wind. She is telling you about a time when she was first married and the snow got so high that it covered up all of the cars on the street, and everyone was stranded, stuck

in their homes for days. You are trying to decide if you believe her when
he walks through the gate. He grins at you, and you smile back, and it
feels like summer.

While Chris is home, you spend every minute you can with him. At
the Christmas Eve service at Deerbrook, you fumble the words of the
Christmas story as you read them on stage. You know he is there, watching you, and the thought makes it difficult to focus on the small typeface
in your Bible.

You exchange gifts by his family's artificial Christmas tree, leaning
up against a pile of fat art books that his dad has checked out from the
library. When Chris gives you a thank-you hug, he pauses, his face hovering near yours. You want to kiss him, but you know it's against Teen
Mania's rules, so instead, you reach out and touch his face. You place your
small hands along the bottom of his jaw and you watch him while he
closes his eyes, inhales deeply.

It is a month marked by happiness, a month draped with so much
glimmering tinsel. When he leaves to go back, you are sad but you feel
strong. You feel as if you have made it through the worst of all of this. You
think that this shining month was maybe enough to get you through the
rest of the year.

But a few days later, the phone rings, and it is Chris calling from
Texas, his voice crackly in the long distance. "I just called to tell you that
I can't talk anymore," he says.

"What?" you say, pressing the plastic receiver to your ear. "Wait…
what?"

"I've sinned," he sighs. "I've *been* sinning. Teen Mania interns are
supposed to break ties with all romantic relationships…and…all that
time we spent together over Christmas…"

"Wait." You stop him, pulling the kitchen telephone away from your
mom's curious gaze and the sound of garlic toast frying on the stove. You
slide into the basement stairwell and shut the door behind you. "I don't
understand. I mean…we saw each other…but we weren't like…*to-*

gether…" You replay his time home in your mind in fast-motion, trying to riddle out what he's saying.

"I've already talked to my team leader about it," Chris says. "He says I need to make a clean break of it…that I can't fully pursue God's will and stay connected to you at the same time." He pauses. "He says that you're causing me to stumble."

"I'm sorry," you say breathlessly.

"I'm sorry too," he says. You hear voices behind him, faraway Texas voices. The voices of the men who know about you, about your relationship, who believe you are a stone that is causing him to fall.

"Look," Chris says, "I have to go."

"Yeah," you say. "Sure, yeah." He hangs up before you can say good-bye.

➤ ◀

You're a little bit weepy on the night that you sit with Felix in the dark of his parked car. It's been a bad time for you. The letters from Chris have stopped coming, just as he said they would. When the phone rings, it is no longer him, standing in the hallway of his dorm, telling you his stories. You have caused him to stumble, so he has kicked you out of the way. You are lonely. Felix is dabbing at the tears on your face with his long fingers. He swallows, and you are close enough to his neck to see the way it makes his Adam's apple move along his throat.

He is a senior, a friend from youth group. He is handsome. He knows that he is handsome. He has good hair and perfect lips and a tall, built body. The girls like Felix and Felix likes the girls and because of this, he has gotten himself into trouble more than once. So in a renewed commitment to personal purity, he has taken his devotion to abstinence to the next level: a dating sabbatical. A break from girls altogether. He is dating Jesus.

Sort of.

Right now, it feels as if he is dating you.

You can't see anything outside of the car, though you know you are in a housing development, one of the rich ones with lots of big trees, lots of little empty turnabouts like the one where you are currently parked. Inside, the numbers on the clock cast a green glow on Felix's sharp features. He leans toward you so that you are forehead to forehead, and you can feel your heart lurching erratically. He stares at you. You stare at him. He moves so close that you can feel the five o'clock shadow poke against your breathless cheeks.

You inhale sharply and back away, and the magic breaks. You put your two small fingers against his lips. "You're dating Jesus, remember?" you say.

That is the truth in this moment—not the beating of your heart against the darkness, but the unbreakable promise to God that forms the context behind it. Felix has vowed not to date girls, and you know what happens when you come between boys and their vows.

Besides, you are supposed to be waiting. Waiting for Chris, who is in Garden Valley, Texas, also dating Jesus, and consequently, not speaking to you. He is fighting the forces of evil and doing great things for the Lord. You are supposed to be quiet, reserved, watching over the horizon for the beginning of happily ever after. Not alone in a dark car with Felix and his perfect lips.

You should have let him kiss you.

If you had, maybe this would not be your story, your journey, your burden. If you had done what you wanted to do instead of watching over the boys and their vows…if you had allowed yourself to be hurt the usual ways that teenage boys hurt teenage girls instead of falling so nobly on the sword of the Spirit, a constant sacrifice, dying again and again to your own desires, then maybe it would not have gone like this.

Nine

I'm Feeling Led: A phrase used to explain decisions, indicating that God has shown you a clear way, and that you are simply following His command. Synonymous phrases include: "God told me to," and "God has put this on my heart..."

I n August, he came home.

He flew in on a Tuesday, and that evening, he was walking toward me on the shore of Lake Michigan. Chris Jacobson, in the flesh, kicking up the sand on Glencoe Beach with his bare feet like the hero in a romance movie. Except that he was not walking toward me *exactly,* he was walking toward all of us—the whole Deerbrook Youth Group. We met at the beach every Tuesday night in the summer to swim, to eat roasted hot dogs, to lob a volleyball back and forth across a net in the sand as dusk fell over the lake.

Chris smiled, gave me a swift side-hug, and then moved on to someone else. He was taking it slow, moving cautiously back into the world outside the Teen Mania headquarters. I imagine there was a fair amount of culture shock involved. Suddenly, he was allowed to hug a member of the opposite sex, to look long into someone's eyes, to let the smile go all the way to his heart. Suddenly, he was allowed to be in love.

It took awhile for this to register. But before long, I was driving my new (used) green Honda along the webbed back roads of the Chicago suburbs, Buffalo Grove bleeding into Lincolnshire into Deerfield. Deerfield, where Trinity International University hid behind Highway 294, a mere seven miles from my house. Chris had enrolled there, and that fall he moved into a big, brick dormitory across from the soccer fields. This was where he would major in missions, where he would *stay,* if I was lucky, for the next few years.

It took awhile for him to say *love* again, but eventually he did.

It was November. I was sixteen. He took my face in his hands and looked me in the eye while we stood under red- and orange-tinted trees on Trinity's campus. He said, "Be my girlfriend."

It was everything I had been waiting for. Of course, I said, "Yes."

Two days later, Chris was grinning in the driver's seat of his black Toyota, driving toward a neighborhood I cannot remember to the house of a boy I cannot name. The boy was a commuter in one of Chris's classes at school. He was small and quiet with dark hair and big glasses. Every week, he went to New Testament class where he sat in the shadow of Chris's charisma. I suppose they talked in the moments before and after class, in the pauses where the teacher asked them to take out their Bibles and turn to the thirteenth chapter of Romans.

And then one day, it was the boy's birthday. I imagine that he sat in class quietly, mustering up the courage because his mother hugged him tight that morning, told him to ask some friends to come to the party. At the end of class, he told Chris that it was his birthday and asked if he would come. Chris smiled big. In his mind, he was already asking me; he was calling our friends, Megan and Brian. We were all piling into the Toyota. We were saving the party.

He was nineteen. He believed in the power of numbers and good intentions. He clapped the kid on the back, shot him that all-American grin. "I'll be there," he said.

Here are the things I remember about the party: The boy's mother in her tiny, dark kitchen. The sound of her Spanish, her arms, reaching through the steam that billowed from the rice pot on the stove. The awkward handshake of the boy who came to the kitchen expecting to see his friend, Chris, and instead found strangers. The mother, swatting him with a worn kitchen towel, saying Spanish words that I imagine meant, "Well? Don't be rude! Invite your friends in!" I imagine he thought, *Friends?*

But he led us down creaky stairs anyway and into the paneled basement where all of his relatives floated like petals on the surface of the linoleum. Warm hands clasped mine while tones of welcome swirled around us. A woman with deep smile lines handed me a plate: sizzling green peppers curled into clumps of sticky rice, which I sort of pretended to eat. Someone crooned in Spanish from a scratchy old record, years after the rest of the world had sprung ahead to cassettes, and then to CDs. Everyone danced.

Chris and I sat on the orange velvet couch while aunts and grandparents and cousins curved fluidly into the cha-cha without ever glancing at their feet. Eyes on eyes, hands brushing the small of the back, rounded, child-bearing hips gliding like grace against the music. I shifted clumsily. I was trying to get Chris to drape his arm across my shoulders or take my hand. Instead, one of the uncles grabbed me by the wrists and pulled me up off the couch. His Spanish slid musically into the sound of the mandolin on the record as he tried to get me to move *forward, back. Cha cha cha.* He laughed. He said words I couldn't understand but could feel like rhythm. *Relax. Loosen up.*

In one fluid movement, he passed me off to Chris, who had stood up, and was now tall and rigid in the middle of the floor. He grabbed my hand tentatively while everyone circled around us. Their laughter mixed with the music as I tried to move the way the uncle taught me. I willed my hips to loosen, but all they knew was the junior high slow dance.

Across from us, Megan and Brian were spinning loose circles around

each other. They both danced in the high school show choir. They were
making it up as they went along.

One, two. Cha, cha, cha.

Chris was rocking *back, forth, back, forth* from right to left foot, legs
locked at the knees. He was as vertical as the poles reaching up to the
ceiling. Around us, bodies opened and closed like flowers. The music
lengthened into a slow ballad, and they were everything natural and soft.

But Chris and I, we were hard angles, jutting awkwardly from the
dance floor. We were looking at our feet, at each other's feet, stepping
sharply on each other's shoes. He clenched his teeth, tightened his hand,
tried to lead me into steps that neither of us knew. *Forward, back...*

— —

Later, in the first whitewashed days of January, Chris took me on a date
to the town Park District. It was a weekday during the winter break, and
the place was quiet. Our steps echoed against the floor as we walked up
the stairs, and I asked again, "What's this all about?" But Chris shook his
head, smiled—it was a surprise. When we got to the registration desk, he
grabbed a pamphlet from it and held it in front of me. "Ta da!"

Ballroom dancing lessons.

I was a junior in high school. My friends' boyfriends were taking
them to Applebee's for dinner, to the boys' basketball game against Ste-
venson. They were taking them to action movies starring Bruce Willis;
they were feeling them up in dark parking lots.

But my boyfriend was in college. He was filling out a registration
form for ballroom dancing lessons. He was browsing the list of dances we
would learn during the eight-week course, reading aloud a description of
the waltz.

So when he looked up from the form and said, "Hey, would you
mind paying for half the registration fee? It's kind of expensive...," I said,
"Of course" and fumbled through my wallet for enough cash while he
wrote the check.

"This is going to be so awesome," Chris said. "We're gonna be expert dancers." He was excited. His words bounced hard against the doors of empty classrooms and escaped down empty hallways.

— —

We learned to ballroom dance in a windowless classroom in the bottom of the Park District building, a room plastered with the art of preschool children. A giant paper sun smiled down at us from the wall, while outside, the January night swirled snowy. We were the youngest couple in the classroom, and we stood with the others in two straight lines: women on one side, men on the other. We passed sweet smiles like notes.

We began with the waltz. There was a portable boom box on the floor playing a hazy duet of violins and violas. It was the kind of song that made you think of pink sequined gowns and top hats. Pin curls. Stars.

I was Doris Day; Chris was Rock Hudson. Life was a musical extravaganza.

The teacher flitted from couple to couple, posing us like Barbie dolls: Chris's hand on my back, my hand reaching up to his right shoulder. *Closed* position. Our teacher was small and spunky. She pushed me into place with her hands. "It's not just about holding hands," she told us. "It's about employing body contact and support. It's about holding each other up." I should know which way to move my feet by the softness of his hand against my back. *One* two three. *One* two three. *Box turn.*

We mastered the basics but had trouble when we got to the underarm turn. I couldn't figure out what my feet should be doing. The teacher tried to show me—"sidestep, close, forward, sidestep, close"—but it was useless; her steps were an accent I could not repeat.

— —

In Texas, Chris's faith had become stronger and sharper. It was systematic and efficient, a complicated choreography that I wanted to learn. Every morning, he read a chapter of the Old Testament; every lunch hour, a psalm. Before bed, it was always something from the New Testament. *Walk-side-close.* Three box turns forming a complete circle of discipline. He led our weekly church Bible study, and I uncapped my pen. As he spoke, I underlined verses in my Bible, wrote his words in the margins, gospel truth.

Sunday nights, he taught our youth group. He took long, smooth steps across the front of the church gym, his Bible propped open in one hand. The boyish smile was gone, replaced with focused intensity. He was a good speaker. He knew how to look around the room and make eye contact with almost everyone there. But when his eyes met mine, they showed no flicker of recognition or love. It was as if they were fixed on a focal point at the back of the gym.

A few weeks after we started dating—before he signed us up for ballroom dancing—he drew up a contract for our relationship and went through it for me point by point at a Barnes and Noble coffee shop. "I think it's important to create firm boundaries so we don't get caught up in a moment," Chris had said. There were eleven or twelve points, most of which I cannot remember. The first involved putting God ahead of our relationship at all times. The second restricted our physical affection to handholding and hugs. There was something about not allowing our relationship to interfere with church and something about reading the Bible together, but I can't remember exactly.

Below he had created several lines for signatures: mine, his, each of our parents', the youth pastor's, and even the head pastor's (a necessity since he was officially a youth-group leader now, and I was a student). When I brought the contract home to my parents, my dad laughed, as if it were a joke. He opened the freezer door and poured a handful of after-dinner chocolate chips into the palm of his hand. When he looked back at me, he had his eyebrows raised. He stared at my careful signature for a minute before conceding. "I think it's stupid, but I'll sign it…if you're sure it's what you want."

I'd been waiting for a year to have Chris this close to me. To feel in my lungs his sharp inhale as he said, "If my life is just a breath, I want to take the biggest gulp of GOD that I can." So I made my body a shadow, moved myself into the closed position. I waited for him to push me forward.

— —

When the first dance class ended, we walked toward the front door. Outside, I could see the snow falling bright against the night sky. I wanted us to walk outside, to stand in the dark, holding hands. My brain was tired of calculating steps; my feet were tired of trying to keep the beat. I wanted to fall like the snow.

But Chris wanted to practice. He led me down the stairs and to an empty basement hallway. "I just think we should get this right before we learn another dance," he said.

We moved into position, worked the basic figure of the waltz: *box turn, box turn, box turn...spin.* I missed the beat.

"Try it again," he said patiently. "It's *one*-two-three...go *under* my arm...let go...now *grab* my hand."

I could feel my shoulders stiffening. I was concentrating hard. One time, I got it right, and Chris grinned and hugged me. The next time, I missed it. "You *had* it," he said. "Again."

I looked deeply into his eyes. I was looking for romance, but he wore his teaching-youth-group face, all intensity and determination. I wanted to move like Ginger to his Fred, like Cinderella to his Prince Charming. But he had to go back to school; he had an exam the next day.

He hugged me fast, told me to practice every day.

— —

That week, he canceled our dinner date to prepare a Bible study, but I said I understood. We talked on the phone in small circles about the particulars of our days. I wanted him to say he loved me, missed me, wished he could blow off his Bible study to be with me. Instead, he said, "I'm thinking about trying to fast for forty days."

"Forty days!" I said, "You'll die!"

"I won't die," he said humorlessly. "Jesus fasted for forty days. I think we should try to do everything Jesus did."

I wanted to say I'd do it with him. I wanted him to believe I was strong and spiritual, able to take big great gulps of God in place of food. But then I thought about *forty days* of nothing but water and said nothing.

I could tell he was disappointed by my lack of solidarity, but I changed the subject anyway, trying to pull our conversation back to the singsong, three-quarter-time talk that is easy, that ends in "I love you," and "I love you."

— —

We learned to fox-trot with the long, jazzy phrases of Frank Sinatra, who, it seemed, had the world on a string. I had still not mastered the waltz, though I had been practicing in my tiny basement bedroom every night. My arms were sore from being propped up against invisible shoulders all week. Even so, I was flustered and couldn't remember any of the steps.

Now there was a new beat involved: *Slow. Slow. Quick-quick.* "Like a fox," the dance instructor said. Or like Harry Fox, the vaudeville actor, who invented the dance out of irritation and necessity because his female partners couldn't grasp the two-step.

The instructor brushed over the basics. The fox trot was similar enough to the waltz, so she moved quickly on to feather turns and promenades, stagger steps and time steps. I stiffened my knees, watched my feet. *Right foot forward; left foot forward; right foot to side; left foot closed.* She came up behind me, pushed my shoulders down with the palms of her hand. "You have to learn to *relax*," she said.

I could feel Chris getting frustrated. He held my hand more firmly. His hand on my back was heavy and forceful. I tried to listen, to breathe, but I felt as though I would never get it. Frank Sinatra felt as though spring had sprung.

Later, the dance instructor used Chris as an example to show the class what a proper feather turn looked like. He put his arm on her back and grinned at her, making small, controlled steps around the classroom. *Slow. Slow. Quick-quick.* I watched his feet, unhindered by my mistakes. His movements were sharp and perfect. He cut across the floor like a knife.

I stood watching them. "Your boyfriend's a natural," a lady next to me said. I nodded and thought about the softness of the dancers at that party a few months ago. I thought about the unstudied look of their cha-cha, the warmth of their breath on my skin as they moved close, said clumsy English *hellos.* I thought about grace: the outstretched arms of the Spanish mother...welcoming...welcoming...

— —

Someone once told me that children are born with the capacity for making any word or sound or accent—born into the possibility of all languages. But somewhere in the constant whir of English words, certain sounds begin to fall away—the rolling *r*'s of French, the rise and fall of Chinese tones—exchanged for words like *eat* and *bye-bye.*

I think about all that has slipped out of me over the years, the untapped potential that glimmered, dimmed, disappeared. I wonder if I once contained the ability to move freely across the dance floor, and if it is still there, a recessive gene lying dormant to dances like the electric slide and the chicken dance. Or is it gone—like an accent, like a breath?

— —

I didn't want to practice after class that night, but I asked, "Do you want to practice?" I knew that if we left the building, I would not see Chris for days. He had meetings all week for an upcoming missions trip to the Ukraine. He had plans and language tapes and a big stack of Ukrainian Bibles.

"Not tonight," he said. "Would you just drop me off at school?"

"Sure," I said. At Trinity, I got out of the car when he did, hoping he would suggest a walk under the bare branches of the elm trees. But he gave me a hug, said, "I love you," and moved steadily up the stairs to his building. I waited, leaning against the green hood of my Honda. I thought that maybe he would turn around at the top of the steps—that he would heel turn and smile at me.

He walked into the building without looking back.

He was thinking, I imagine, about his trip to the Ukraine and about love: the bigness of it, the unpredictability of it. He was thinking about his parents and of all the stories he'd heard: men destined for great things, men who traded it all for the soft hand of a girl. He was so afraid he would spin out of control. One lingering moment, one step out of line, and he would be trapped.

He could feel me waiting for him, I think, waiting for a smile, a wave, a look. But he kept in step. He moved steadily through the door, kept his eyes on the focal point at the back of his mind.

— —

That week, his calls came in stagger steps. I spent two slow nights reading a novel while the cordless phone lay lifeless beside my bed. Saturday and Sunday, his calls came in quick spurts. He had a cold and couldn't get together over the weekend. He probably wouldn't be able to make it to ballroom dancing Monday night to learn the cha-cha. He hoped I understood.

"Of course," I said. "Can I bring you some soup or something?"

But he didn't want soup. "I think I'm just going to sleep all day. Maybe read my Bible a little."

Monday and Tuesday passed slowly. I wandered from class to class, feather-turning excuses in my mind.

— —

The next two weeks were rocky with silence. Silence mounting into tension, tension mounting into rage and tears. For two and a half years, I'd been unquestioningly devoted to Chris, but in reality, we'd only dated for four months.

I could tell it was over. I knew it in my deepest heart, felt it like light changing around me. I cried. I raged. And then I planned one last-ditch effort: an elaborate celebration for Chris's twentieth birthday.

We would go ice-skating at our favorite park, have a picnic. I made a mixed tape and borrowed a portable stereo. For an hour, I stood outside in my jacket and mittens, rigging up the trunk of my car so that when he opened it, balloons would fly out and a sign would pop up: *Happy Birthday!*

An hour before he was supposed to come over, he called to cancel. He had a Bible study thing that he really needed to do.

"No," I said.

"What?"

"I said *no*, Chris." I tried to steady my voice. "I planned all of this stuff for your birthday. You have to come over. We had *plans*."

"Fine," he said, his breath hard against the receiver. "Whatever. I'll be there in a while."

He came. We drove to the ice rink in Arlington Heights, and I opened the trunk of the car. My sign had gotten a little squished by the picnic basket. The balloons had shrunk from the cold. Chris smiled politely and thanked me anyway. We skated for ten minutes before he told me that the skates I'd borrowed for him must have been the wrong size. He had blisters. He was ready to go.

━ ━

The night we were supposed to learn the tango, I called him from my after-school job at Hair Sensations salon to see if he wanted to have dinner before class. "I guess," he said.

We met at the McDonald's on Deerfield Road. He was late. I waited idly by the ketchup pumps and napkin canisters for ten minutes before finally ordering, and then I ate french fries slowly and watched for him out the window. When he finally came, he didn't order, just slid into the chair across from me.

"Aren't you going to get something?" I asked.

"Nope. Already ate."

"Well, then, why did you say you'd meet me for dinner?"

He shrugged. *Fine,* I thought. I ate quietly. He scrutinized my face for a few moments, then said, "You know, you'd be a lot prettier if you got rid of all of those blackheads on your nose."

— —

He gave me a cardboard kaleidoscope once—during that first year, before Texas, before we were "dating." He'd made it in art class out of an old Pringles can, and then he spent the next week embellishing the outside with fluid green lines.

"What's this for?" I asked, surprised when he handed it to me. We were sitting on a park bench, eating Subway sandwiches.

Chris looked down, reddened slightly around the ears. "It just…it reminded me of you."

I tilted the kaleidoscope toward the light, turned the end, watched as the beads filtered into place, falling into different configurations of color and light. "It's beautiful!"

"Just like you," he said.

I smiled and turned the kaleidoscope again…thought nothing of it when the beads slipped away from the light, disappeared.

— —

I knew that I should break up with him when he said the thing about the blackheads. But it seemed so strange, so unlike him, this blatant meanness, this hateful moment. So I blinked back the tears.

He back-pedaled a bit, made a hasty cover-up, an insincere apology.

I nodded and excused myself to go to the ladies' room, where I splashed cold water on my stinging eyes. There was no time to be mad. We had to learn the tango: two long, smooth steps, then a sharp turn outward. Promenade. Sidestep, sidestep, sidestepping issues as we turned around the room. From the boom box, horns slid along the gamut of emotions—anger, passion, love, anger again—percussion rattled like a snake.

I was not getting the steps right, but it didn't seem to matter anymore. We spent the evening trying to figure out the oversway…and, more difficult, how to recover from it. *Right foot side, flex knee. Recover weight. Promenade. Tap step.*

I didn't want to think about flexing my right knee. I wanted to dance the way they did in the movies: one moment, so close that noses are almost touching, the next, turning abruptly away. I wanted to say things with my body that I could not say with my mouth, things that were not part of the steps we were learning, had learned, would ever learn.

Step. Step. TURN.

I wanted to be among those who danced the tango in the dark, black streets of Argentina. I wanted to step into the slums of Buenos Aires before the tango was brought to France…before *The Sunshine Girl* launched the simple dance into fame. I wanted to go back to dance when it was not about steps but about life. Tango as gospel. Tango as faith—as reaching for something in the dark. Moving because we are moved, because there is nothing else to do but move, but to curve into one another…welcoming each other through the steam.

I wanted to go through an entire dance lesson and not learn one step because I was laughing too hard, because I was dancing with someone I loved, and we were being pulled across the rhythms by something strong and profound.

Step. Step. TURN.

I wanted to breathe the music in through my nose; to try to get all of my senses around it. I wanted it to be something inside of me. Something like love, something like grace.

Step.

Step.

Turn.

— • —

At the end of class that night, Chris hugged me hard, then turned sharp from our relationship. He ignored me for three days, and then, on the Friday before Valentine's Day, he called at two in the morning. "I've been praying about this a lot," he said as I struggled, groggy, to sit up in my bed. He took a deep breath, an exhale, and then, "I feel like God is telling me to break up with you."

We broke up after Week Four of ballroom dancing class. We never learned the merengue or the rumba or the mambo. We did not learn to swing.

On the phone that night, I focused on breathing, on drawing the air into my lungs and holding it there. Somehow, I knew that it would not be like the other breakups and nonbreakups. He would not be coming back this time.

I didn't argue, though I recall being angry. I could not think of a way to question his word from God. I remember waiting for him to say something else, anything else…even "Let's just be friends." But he didn't, and I didn't offer. It was as if we both knew that friendship was an accent from the too-distant past. Gone. Lost. Impossible to relearn.

— • —

We broke up for lots of reasons. Mostly, we broke up because a year before, Chris ran from our shared world, and he watched with rapt attention while some teacher in Texas stood in front of a podium and broke faith into a hundred little steps. Kneel on your floor at the beginning of the day and pray. Do not move until you receive a word from God. Read your Bible three times every day. Memorize at least one verse—*walk, side, close.* Go to faraway countries. Speak the name of Jesus loud on street corners.

We broke up because his faith had become an axis of rotation around which no one could freely turn. It was the vertical line that cut through the center of his body, through his feet, his heart, out the center of his head and into the sky. It was the horizontal line, pulling us taut, keeping us far from each other. It was a hundred small perfect steps that in the end can never add up to dance...not the kind I wanted, anyway. Not the tango of Argentina, of the Spanish birthday party.

If I had it to do over again, I would have stayed on that crowded basement floor with the uncle a bit longer. I wouldn't have tried so hard to follow his feet.

And then, when he tried to pass me over to Chris, I like to think that I would have walked right by him, walked over to where Megan and Brian were spinning circles, to where they were laughing, to where they were making it up as they went along.

If I had it to do over again, I would have danced like Buenos Aires.

I'd be a helicopter leaf, a snowflake falling. I would have stayed there spinning wild and lovely across the dark, lonely sky.

Ten

Let Go and Let God: A bumper-sticker phrase given when there is no easy answer. In difficult situations, one is advised to give up control and surrender to God.

C hris is such a jerk," Kim said in disgust, unbuckling and turning sideways in the middle seat of the church van so she could see me better in the back.

"Seriously," Alissa agreed, rolling her eyes.

It was the day after The Breakup Phone Call, and I'd spent the morning in bed, my mom quietly calling the school secretary to say that I would not be coming to classes that morning, I needed to take a sick day.

But it was afternoon now, and long before the breakup I'd committed to this weekend mission trip. We were headed to a battered women's shelter in Springfield, Illinois, and it was too late to back out. So I met my friends at the high school driveway that afternoon and bumbled into the backseat of the church van.

They had hugged me hard and close. They'd asked, "Are you okay?" And I'd said, "Sure, fine," though, in truth, I was having trouble with everyday activities: putting one foot in front of the other, breathing in and out, talking and eating and drinking things down.

Alissa looped her arm through mine as the van rushed toward Springfield. "Someone needs to hit him over the head with a wok."

"A wok?" I asked, eyebrows raised, but I knew her well enough to know that this was evangelical for *What an asshole.*

Kim passed a bag of M&M'S back to us. "Here. Eat these. Chocolate makes everything better."

"I don't think I can," I said, knowing that I looked pale and gaunt and as if I could use an M&M or two. I could see a patch of my face in the rearview mirror, but I hardly recognized it. It was blotchy with sadness; puffy from crying. The relationship had lasted two and a half years in one form or another—not actually that long, except if you are in high school, and it is your first love. Then two and a half years is an ocean, and when the relationship capsizes, you find yourself going down with it.

"You don't have to eat them," Alissa said. "Just throw them. Throwing things always makes you feel better."

The wife of the youth pastor turned back from the driver's seat. "Please don't throw food in my van, girls."

"Out the window, then."

"Yes." Kim opened the bag and poured some M&M'S into my hand while Alissa turned to the window next to her. When she tried to open it, we realized it was one of those windows that doesn't actually roll down, but rather pushes out an inch so that a small puff of breeze can slither through.

"Well, this is going to be tricky," Alissa said as the breeze played at the ends of her brown hair. She took a green M&M in her hand and tried to lob it through the tiny opening. "Take that, Chris!" she said vehemently. The M&M bounced off the wall of the van and disappeared under the backseat.

"Well done," said Kim, shaking her head, her long red braid swaying against her back.

"Shoot."

"Let me try," Kim said. She grabbed a red M&M out of the bag. "This is for all of those times that he made you wait around for him." She chucked it toward the window opening, and it clinked against the glass and disappeared, falling to the rolling road beneath us. "And that's how it's done, girls."

"Whatever. I need to try again." Alissa grabbed a handful of M&M'S. "Strength in numbers," she added when I raised an eyebrow. I let out a hoarse laugh, and Kim and Alissa let it pass, unmarked. None of us had learned, yet, that evangelical tendency to package things up tidily. To chirp at one another, "God never gives you more than you can handle!" Or "Everything happens for a reason!" Or "Let go and let God!"

Instead, they worked in subtle, slow ways to help me redefine the memory of this relationship, to see that it was not The One, to understand that I could recover. They were trying to help me navigate a new normal, but they knew better than to actually say any of it out loud. So they threw the M&M'S. At sixteen, this is how you do the quiet, patient work of caring for battered souls.

"All right," Alissa said. "This is for the time he told you that if you wanted to be with him, you had to give birth in a hut in the desert."

"Jungle." I corrected her with a slow nod.

"That's right," she said. "For the hut in the African jungle." She shook her head and then sent a handful of candies streaking toward the window. They rattled off, bouncing wildly through the backseat. The youth pastor's wife pursed her lips in the rearview mirror.

"I am the worst M&M thrower on the planet," Alissa said, kicking a few chocolates backward under the seat where the youth pastor's wife couldn't easily see them.

"What do you think?" Kim asked tentatively.

I reached into the bag silently and took a blue M&M. I understood, as I held that chocolate between my fingers, that this was not so much a symbol as it was a small catharsis. A tiny blue beginning. I knew that I would not be able to let go of all of this the way I could let go of a piece of candy. That this whole thing was lodged deep, and really, this was nothing but an M&M. But still. It was *something*.

"For two and a half *years*," I said, hurling the M&M toward the window. The girls hooted behind me as it rebounded off the glass and slipped quietly away.

Part Two

Disillusion

Eleven

Calling: A God-appointed task. A weighty, spiritual reason for pursuing a specific vocation, ministry, or mission.

The next missionary boy was Nick Garcia, and he was beautiful: curly black hair, long eyelashes, one of *those* smiles. People were always putting us together, looking at the two of us side by side as if they were appraising our value as a couple. As if they were picturing our future children. Sometimes I found myself doing the same thing, drifting away from myself and watching us as we stood together at his mother's sink, washing the dishes after a Bible study meeting.

For a fleeting moment, I'd wonder if I could end up with him in Norway, the country where he planned to be a missionary. He would have a flat there, and stylish European kids with chunky black glasses and tight leather jackets would sit in a circle in his living room, listening to him talk about God on dark Norwegian nights. I tried to imagine myself there with him, holding a ceramic mug, part of his glamorous missionary world.

It had been more than a year since the breakup with Chris, and I'd recovered in that patchy way that you do from a first love. I'd learned to ignore his continued presence as a leader in our youth group; I'd learned to say a cordial hello to him in the church foyer.

I'd started dating other boys.

I spent a blissful summer before my senior year of high school as a counselor at an evangelical camp, where I kissed dark-skinned Calvin under the hazy moon. I hardly knew him at all; I only knew that he was

handsome and that I wanted to see what it was like—to kiss someone just
for the fun of it, without a three-page contract, without any thought of
marriage. I was surprised at how detached I could remain, even with my
lips on his at a camp picnic table in the summer dark. He was just some
guy. I was just a girl. It was just a kiss.

In the fall, I briefly dated a friend's older brother. He was in college
and had eyes the color of robin's eggs. I'd broken things off with him
when I learned that he planned to work at the John Deere plant and live
out in the country. Even though Chris and I had broken up, I knew I was
still meant to be *someone's* missionary wife. I was leading three Bible studies; I was driving freshman girls to youth group events and to that punk-
rock youth church, Vertical Impact. I was telling them not to settle for an
ordinary life while I gazed pensively across the sky into my blurry future.
They were writing me notes, these high school girls, notes that said, "You
are such a woman of God!!" "You are going to do GREAT THINGS for the
LORD!"

I didn't know where; I just knew that I would *go*. I had claimed for
myself an extraordinary future; I had done it years ago as I sat on a swing
and stared up at the wide, starry sky. I was meant to leave all this behind.

Nick Garcia was going to be a missionary. He was already enrolled
in a program; he already had an airplane ticket. We had known each
other since our sophomore year of high school, when we both attended a
meeting at Vertical Impact. We had become instant friends and had
stayed close, mostly because our lives seemed to move inexplicably in
tandem. We were always in serious relationships at the same time—me,
on-and-off with Chris, him with a series of sweet punk-rock girls. And
we were always shoring up side by side, bruised and waterlogged after the
relationships went down.

The spring of our senior year, we were both single. When we graduated, he would go to Norway for missionary training school, and I would
go to Minnesota to college. But we careened together anyway through

the endless spring days, drinking vanilla-flavored coffee, making plans for prom, not ever talking much about the leaving.

He left for Norway in June, just after we graduated. There was a garbled message from the airport terminal on my answering machine when I got home that summer morning. "I was hoping I would get to say good-bye to you," the message had said. "I was hoping you would be there." His voice had a solemn quality that pierced the static, and I felt bad that I hadn't been in the cool of my basement bedroom when the phone rang to tell him that it was okay. That he could go. That he was always going to go.

— —

To understand what happened to me when I went to college, you have to first understand this: I *let him go,* this missionary boy. I did it purpose-fully, willfully. I was healing from that excruciating breakup with Chris; the broken places in me were fusing together stronger than before.

On a youth group trip to Tennessee at the end of my senior year, I had scaled the sharp wall of the Smoky Mountains, and it had been sur-prisingly easy to find the footholds, to see the next rock to grab. Chris had been behind me, along with us on the trip as a leader. His breath was shallow and shaky as he tried to steady his feet on the wall. "Can you wait for me?" he'd asked, and I'd replied sweetly, "Of course." But I hadn't waited. I was stronger than that now. I climbed faster, more intentionally, climbed ahead of him toward the top.

To understand my story, you have to know that the spring of my senior year, I found my voice. Nick and I sat together that April in the late-night fluorescence of an empty Dunkin' Donuts, drinking coffee, talking about Norway. He was trying to tell me that he wanted me to wait for him but that he would never ask it of me, and the conversation felt dramatic and urgent. It felt like That Moment in a movie, and I could have gone the way of the movie girls. But I was intoxicated on spring.

Graduation was only a few weeks away and life felt spacious around me. I was swept up in the momentum of all of the good-byes; I was high off all the letting go.

"We'll be friends," I'd said calmly. "We'll always be friends." I'd learned the hard way about waiting for a boy. I was stronger now. Harder. A little more careful with my great, wide love. I did not even try to hold on to the slippery edges of the relationship when he left. I released it. And in doing so, I felt a sudden freedom to reinvent myself. I had an entire summer to do it, and when the summer was over, I would drive up through the Midwest and start entirely over.

— • —

I attended a college in Minnesota called Northwestern. It was a small evangelical liberal arts school tucked in the crease between Saint Paul and Minneapolis. I chose Northwestern for lots of reasons that I don't remember and some that I do. When I chose it, I was half sunk into my senior year. I was just starting to recover from the breakup, and I realized all at once I was so *tired*. I'd spent the last four years defending a faith I was sure was being attacked. Teachers were forever trying to get me to believe in evolution or take a handful of condoms for the premarital sex I most definitely would not be having. I was tired of the *spiritual battle*. Tired of being a *prayer warrior,* of wielding the *sword of the Spirit,* of donning *the armor of God.* These are the evangelical clichés—orphaned from their greater biblical context—that formed the wartime ethic in which I'd lived my life since the day I met Chris.

And while I had become unquestionably stronger over the last year, I was just so *tired* of all this fighting. I wanted to be somewhere safe, and the idea of evangelical school felt like rest to me. I imagined myself warmed by the light of thousands of students, all holding out a small, strong flame for Christ. I imagined the intimacy of instant family that I'd felt on youth group retreats and certain mission trips and at camp, only I saw it amplified, echoing in all the dark and lonely places of my heart.

The first unexpected twist at Northwestern was my roommates. I walked into our sweltering dorm room that first day, and there they were with their boxes and suitcases and mountains of clothes. Their dads were building their loft beds, and they were eyeing me cautiously as I came lumbering in with all of my baggage.

There is a picture of the three of us from orientation week. We are sitting in our RA's room, holding cookies in our hands. We have milk mustaches. We have only just begun to live together, and we don't know one another yet. Heather's hair is long and blond; Jill's is short and brown, flipped out in layers under her chin; they are both wearing khaki pants and plaid shirts. I am still in summer clothing: a blue tank top, frayed jean shorts. I look sun-bleached and tired and a little out of place.

But in the picture, we are smiling; we are leaning into each other; you could almost mistake us for the great friends I imagined we would be. You could imagine us up all night talking in our pajamas, sprawled over threadbare garage sale furniture, sharing the sordid details of our past lives while eating ice cream from the carton and watching *Friends*. You could *almost* see it: all three of us shoved together in front of our vanity mirror, applying makeup at the same time, mouths open in concentration as we brushed on mascara, lipstick, sparkly eye shadow.

The real Heather and Jill turned out to be nothing like the roommates that I'd created in my head. Real Heather was homeschooled by aging, ailing parents. She wore printed sweaters and sensible boots. She went to bed at ten o'clock every night in flannel pajamas. When she did homework, she sat up straight at her desk, her posture perfect, her hair hanging straight down her back. She never sprawled, never slouched, never tapped her pencil or bit her nails or threw her environmental science book on the floor the way I did. I imagined that in her room at home, she had shelves and shelves of horse figurines.

Real Jill grew up in Colorado Springs where, as I recall, her father worked for Focus on the Family—Dr. James Dobson's family values organization. She was dutiful. Quiet. She studied art and worked slowly and deliberately on her charcoal sketches. The lines she drew mirrored the world she saw perfectly, never altering it, never sharpening what was curved, never exaggerating a point. She rarely left the room. She had a boyfriend back home, and she tapped out conversations with him over her computer instant messenger every night for exactly one hour before she tucked herself into bed.

Heather and Jill immediately set about decorating the dorm room. They had Ideas. Though they were strangers to each other, their tastes and styles and personalities synced perfectly, as though they had been earmarking the same pages of *Martha Stewart Living* all along. As if they had been compiling a joint music collection (Christian Contemporary with flourishes of dulcet piano compilations). They picked a color scheme for our room and hung matching, fabric-covered bulletin boards to tastefully house their photographs. One day they came home from a trip to the craft store with a segment of white picket fence, which they set on our windowsill and covered in stiff, artificial ivy.

At one time, I may have fit exactly right into their world, but I had spent the summer redefining myself. I had been broken, and I had let go of the missionary boy, and I had set about assembling a new identity. I had acquired an eclectic set of thrift-store dishes in different colors and shapes and sizes, dishes with cracks that spoke to me. I had a collection of distinctly outdated thrift sweaters that made me feel unique and edgy. I had spent the summer venturing cautiously into the world of secular music, and I had a pile of mixed CDs featuring bands I'd never heard of. I was infatuated with Coldplay's "Yellow" and with Train's "Drops of Jupiter" and with Rufus Wainwright's rendition of "Hallelujah." I was learning to love new sounds and textures. I was at the part of self-exploration where you have to be surrounded with miscellanea in all of its diversity in order to figure things out.

But Heather and Jill were color-coordinating things and spritzing flower-scented air freshener around the room. They were looking with marked disdain as I taped photographs, askew and unframed, on the brick over my desk. As I screwed the bulb into my kitschy red desk lamp and threw my handmade T-shirt quilt over my bed. When I played my newly created music compilations in our shared CD player, they found their way to their respective desks and quietly put in their ear buds.

During that week of orientation, I spent a lot of time outside, out of the way of my roommates. I walked around the old, beautiful architecture of the campus: stone columns and stained glass and a bell tower that rose regally from Nazareth Hall, looking out over Lake Johanna. I remember feeling in flux. Around me, students filed by, and I watched them. I felt very aware that there were *twenty-five hundred* students at Northwestern, most of them Bible study leaders and prayer group leaders and small group leaders from high school youth groups around the country. Students just like me. We were all jammed onto a small campus with one small road snaking through it, connecting everything.

I remember realizing that I would have to vie for what used to be my most defining characteristic: my faith. The spectrum would be defined differently now; there would be a new "top" and a new "bottom." After all, we couldn't all lead Bible studies here. We couldn't all be RAs or sing in the worship band. Orientation week would end, and the school year would start, and we would filter into new roles. The most spiritual of us would rise to the top; the rest would fall somewhere in the nondescript middle, trying to make our way.

Whether this was a true assessment of evangelical college culture, I still don't know. But I'd spent four years in high school looking for a way to stand apart for the Lord. I'd been standing, all this time, alone at a flagpole, waiting for someone to take my picture. It occurred to me all at once that there would be students here more devout, more spiritual. And that, in addition, they would probably have better clothes, longer legs, fuller hair. It occurred to me that I could not measure up.

I remember spreading a blanket on the grass by a tree on those summer afternoons. The lake was sparkling in the late August sun, sunlight filtering through the tree branches and dancing along its surface, but I was angled away from it, leaning against the tree, my body turned toward the students passing by. I had my Bible open in my lap, and I was sort of reading it, but I was also looking up every few minutes to see if anyone was watching. I was trying to say, *I'm Open*, trying to say, *I'm Available*, trying to say, *Please, look at me.*

— —

"My roommates hate me." I flopped down on the futon in Kim's room. Although Alissa had ended up in Decatur, Illinois, at an artsy school for musical types, Kim had made the trek with me up to Minnesota and lived just a few hallways down in Northwestern's freshman dorm. We had chosen not to room together, afraid that such a close proximity would damage our friendship, but I spent a considerable amount of time sprawled across her futon as though it were a therapist's couch, while she sat at her desk, tapping her pen and nodding sympathetically.

"I know," Kim said, finishing something on her computer and then swiveling toward me on her desk chair. "What did they do now?"

I tossed a CD at her and she caught it in her hands. "They hate the Dixie Chicks?"

"I guess so," I said. "I had it playing, and then I went to the bathroom, for like two seconds…"

"They took your CD out? Now that's just passive-aggressive."

"Yep. It was on my desk when I got back. Jim Brickman is playing now."

"Again?" Kim shook her head.

I yelled into my hands, exasperated. "Also," I said when I emerged from my hand-cave, "they put up more tulle."

Kim's eyes went wide. For a week, Heather and Jill had been fixated on the filmy white material. They had been buying it by the yard from

JoAnn Fabrics and hanging it everywhere. Yesterday, they'd found a way to wrap it around strings of white Christmas lights and loop it over our ceiling. They kept making not-so-subtle suggestions about the photo collage by my bed. They kept putting coasters underneath my cans of Diet Coke.

"I feel like I'm living inside a wedding dress," I said mournfully.

"We *so* should've lived together," Kim said.

The truth is, it happens all the time with roommates. It is nobody's fault, except perhaps the man who decided that three girls could ever coexist happily in one room. We did not click, we did not become best friends, and it would have been fine, except that at evangelical college, everything takes on a spiritual dimension, an added weight.

Instead of saying, "I don't like your music," my roommates said, "Don't you think this CD is kind of...*trashy*? Do you really think God would want you to listen to a song called 'Sin Wagon'?" They grabbed their Bibles and headed to the hall Bible study; they looked at me where I sat on my bed, critiquing papers for a writing class. "Aren't you coming?" they asked. And when I said, "I have so much to do tonight. You guys go on without me," they raised their eyebrows in tandem.

It wasn't Heather's or Jill's fault that I had come to Northwestern a little tired, a little broken, a little unsure of who I was. They didn't understand what it meant when they looked with disdain at my proud collection of thrift sweaters and mismatched picture frames and cracked dishes. How could they know that it had taken only two girls to welcome me into the evangelical world all those years ago in junior high? That just as easily, two girls could push me away from it?

—•—

The second unexpected thing to happen was that I met a missionary boy on the way back from class one day. It was early in the year, and I was still intrigued by all the strange new faces, trying to sort them out, trying to categorize them in my mind. I was interested, especially, in the boys. I was not saying so, but I was on the lookout for The One. I was making mental notes. I was eyeing the ministry majors with their leather camp bracelets and hairy legs and spiritual ambitions.

It was during this time that I met Jared, a tall, blond boy who caught up with me on the way back from freshman seminar one day. We walked together for a stretch of space, hands in our pockets, backpacks slung over our shoulders.

"So," he asked, as we rounded the curve of the sidewalk and came up on the dorm buildings, "what's your major?"

"English. How about you?"

"Missions," he said, a sort of confident finality in his voice. "I'm pretty sure I'm called to the Middle East. Or maybe Africa."

And then he gave me That Look. The one that says, *Hey there. Want to live in a hut in the jungle with me?*

It was as if a warning siren had gone off suddenly, coursing shrilly through my head. *Run!* I felt stunned by this response, so sudden and visceral. It jerked me sharply out of small talk mode as if someone had whacked a hidden reflex with a mallet. All of a sudden it was so clear: I did not want to live in a hut in the jungle. With *anybody*.

"This is my entrance," I said, pointing to the door at the far end of the dorms, although, truth be told, it was not my entrance at all.

"Okay," he said, lingering for a moment. "Well, I hope I see you around." He flashed me a wide grin, the kind shared among missionary boys the world over.

"Yeah," I lied over my shoulder. "Sure. Me too."

I hurried to my room where Heather and Jill were both sitting in their beds, reading their Bibles, while Jim Brickman's piano solos played. They glanced up, and then, when they saw it was me, looked back down. They did not say, *Hey there.* They did not say, *Gee, you look pale.* They did not give me a chance to vocalize what had just occurred to me for the first time ever: I did not want to be a missionary wife. Not at all.

"What are you doing?" Heather finally asked, looking up at me.

"Nothing," I said. "I just realized that I have to go." I turned in the doorway, letting the door close loudly behind me.

— • —

The third unexpected thing to happen was that a plane crashed into a building. And then another one. And then another one.

I spent most of September 11, 2001, sitting in the Northwestern student center, watching the news footage on the large projection screen that someone had rigged against the east wall. I watched the World Trade Center fall and fall and fall again. I was thinking about the fact that this crime was somebody's *mission*. That these acts of violence were done by boys who had planned this carefully, who had boarded the flights early that morning knowing they would not walk again on the sad, broken earth.

I was turning the phrase in my mind. They were not "missionary boys," the pilots of these planes, but they were boys. They were on a mission. Their mission was death that would take others to their death, death big enough to speak a Message to the American people and to the world. I wasn't comparing the missionary boys I knew to terrorists; it was clear to me that something had broken in these men that had caused them to see humans as disposable. But I couldn't seem to stop thinking about the word *mission*. I was aware, suddenly, of the heaviness of it, the electric charge of it, the all-consuming nature.

Someone slid down next to me against the wall.

A boy.

The boy.

I'd met him once before, walking home from a class. He had introduced himself as an international business major. He had talked about his marketing class, where he'd learned the secret to using mnemonic devices for remembering people's names. "Do you have one for me?" I'd asked him coyly as we walked. I admired his blue eyes and the way his long dimples arched deep into his cheeks.

"Yes," he'd said without looking up from the sidewalk. His hair was wild and curly, his face shaved smooth.

"Well, what is it?"

He smiled, first at the sidewalk. Then up at me. "I'm not going to tell you that."

His name was Andrew. He was handsome. He was not a missionary boy.

"Pretty unbelievable," he said that night as we stared at the projector screen.

"I know," I whispered back. We sat there. Our first real conversation, silence. It was boy meets girl and girl meets boy and the vague beginnings of love in the midst of a world that was crashing down around us. It was the end. It was the beginning.

—◆—

At first it was cautious. It was sitting in the student center after classes on weekday afternoons, pretending to study, hoping that Andrew would walk through on his way back to his dorm. It was keeping the volume turned way up on my computer speakers, so that if he pinged me on the instant messenger at eleven thirty at night while I was making a Totino's pizza, I wouldn't miss it.

It was a first date to Como Zoo and a second date to The Buck, the cheap theater on Larpenteur, where the floors were sticky under your shoes and the whole place smelled like stale popcorn.

It was a booth we ran at a local church's fall festival/Halloween alternative. We went dressed as a dog and a cat. He sat still in the student center while I rubbed brown face paint along the creases of his face, into his dimples, over his bushy eyebrows. He let me paint whiskers with eyeliner. "I feel ridiculous," he mumbled as I rubbed a black circle onto his nose. "You look perfect." I grinned. When I did, my white cat face paint cracked in all the right places.

But mostly, in the beginning, it was long walks. We took to the outdoors, and we stayed there, even as fall gave way to the shocking cold of Minnesota winter. Inside, men and women were not allowed in each other's dorm rooms except during weekly visiting hours—small windows of time in which mingling was allowed.

Even then, RAs roamed two by two through the hallways, wandering into dorm rooms. Doors were propped open with wooden wedges, a requirement for hosting someone of the opposite sex. It was one of the RAs' responsibilities to keep an eye on things, to guard against temptation. They tried to be delicate for the most part, but they had to do their job. They had to make sure that all four feet were on the floor while you were cuddled up together on the couch watching a movie; they had to keep an eye out for compromising positions.

Inside, Northwestern functioned strictly within predefined boundaries. But outside, the world was ours.

It was cold, but we wore layers. We met in the dorm stairwell, wearing puffy winter coats over lighter jackets over sweaters over long-sleeved T-shirts over long underwear. Hats. Boots. Scarves.

Glove in glove, Andrew and I walked across the dark campus, the streetlamps casting a muted light on the snow. We were dark shadows, creating powdery pathways where our boots shuffled off the sidewalks and toward Lake Johanna. The water pounded like drums as we slid over the rough, winter-pocked surface. We walked the ridges of the snow, stopping in the moonlight to stare silently into each other's faces, icy breath billowing between us.

We walked.

We walked.

We walked.

"How's your Walk?" my concerned RA, Christy, asked one day. She wasn't asking about the evenings with Andrew—not directly. She was asking about the state of my spirituality, my "walk with God." It was part of her job to enforce the Lifestyle Statement we'd signed upon entering the school. She was on the lookout for new piercings (not allowed), for a faint scent of alcohol on breath (definitely not allowed), for the muffled sound of a boy's voice inside a closed dorm room (forbidden). She had heard from my roommates that I was out late, that I was coming in at two in the morning, red from the cold. That I was in love.

And so she caught up with me on the way to class, her brisk steps matching mine, the snowing crunching beneath us, our backpacks strapped over puffy winter coats.

"It's fine," I told her re: my Walk with the Lord. "Really good."

"That's good," Christy said. She was all brown hair and sincerity. "It can be hard, you know, when the Bible is like, your *textbook*." She was referencing the Bible classes required at Northwestern: a class on the Gospels, one on Paul's Epistles, Old Testament. Evangelism. Theology. It all formed the biblical backbone upon which the rest of our liberal arts education would hinge.

"Sure," I agreed.

"But you know, that doesn't make it any less important to spend time with the Lord," she plowed on. We were walking past the tennis courts, frosted over and abandoned for the winter. I shoved my hands to the bottom of my coat pockets and looked over the heads of the students directly in front of us to see if Andrew's curly hair was up ahead.

"One thing I do is I have this plastic baggy," she continued, oblivious to my distractedness. "And I write Bible verses on note cards and I put them inside of it, and then I *hang it in the shower*." She smiled big, pleased with her creativity. "That way, I can dwell on God's Word while I'm getting ready in the morning."

She looked at me with wide, expectant eyes, so I said something like, "That's a great idea," while glancing behind me to see if Andrew was in the pack of stragglers.

"I have one for you, if you want."

"Sure," I said, gritting my teeth into a smile. She was trying so hard to be helpful. She was a good RA, and she was trying to hand me a lifeline in case I was falling. But I read a subtext in her words that may or may not have actually been there. When she said, "How's your walk?" I heard suspicion. Relationships at Northwestern were a mixed bag: good, in theory, but decidedly tricky. Marriage was the unspoken end game, so much so that a giant boulder near the dorms weekly bore the names of students recently engaged. (*Rebekah + Tim = Forever* was scrawled there that day in blue spray paint, little hearts floating around it.) Matrimony was definitely the goal…but the path to that holy union was treacherous, marked by dark walking paths and darker desires.

I remember this moment so clearly because of the response it evoked when I felt my faith being questioned, felt myself slipping down the spectrum. Her wary look seemed to speak of conclusions she had already reached. I wished she could touch my hand and see my history unfold in a quick succession of images. I wanted her to *see* that I had been a Bible study leader. I wanted her to see me anointing the Prayer Table at school, see me waiting so faithfully for Chris, see me putting my small fingers on Felix's lips that night in the car when he almost kissed me. I wanted her to feel what I felt, to understand that I had been fighting so long to prove myself and I was *tired*. I was just looking for a little rest.

But she couldn't see that. And I couldn't bring myself to tell this history, to turn to her and say, "Look, this is what it was like for me. This is who I am." I was angry and I was defiant, and so I said nothing. I took the rotten Bible Verse Baggie from her and tossed it into my backpack, where it remained for months, crushed by textbooks and notebooks and my Bible as I walked to and from classes.

Christmas came and we all filtered away, disappearing back to the edges of our old lives. Before we left, Andrew and I exchanged Christmas presents in the dormitory stairwell. He gave me a small gold heart necklace, clasped it around my neck while my heart beat wildly in my chest. We promised to e-mail every day.

I came home from Minnesota. Nick, that dark-haired missionary boy, came home from Norway. We hadn't really kept in touch over the semester except for a couple of e-mails, one hastily scrawled postcard, and a fuzzy and unexpected long-distance call. But we met one afternoon over winter break at a small table in the Barnes and Noble coffee shop to catch up. Outside, snowflakes whipped across the wind, and people steeled themselves against the cold as they walked from their cars to the store, pulling their hats over their ears, zipping their coats to the very top.

I can still see us there—a silent film. Nick is nineteen and handsome in his fitted jacket, his cap angled carefully on the top of his black curls. He looks different. Older. A little ragged and pale from soldiering alone through a new country. There are circles underneath his eyes, which are locked on mine, all anticipation and hope.

To be fair, I don't think he meant to propose that day. He meant to say, "I love you." Perhaps he had practiced it over and over in his head; he had hoped it would be enough. But when I fingered the small gold heart pendant hanging around my neck, a necklace from someone else entirely, he realized it wasn't. He would have to up the stakes.

There was no ring, of course, no kneeling down, just a whisper. "Marry me. Come to Norway. I love you."

I can see myself—eighteen years old. My hair is short, lopped off at my ears just before I left for college. I'm wearing a thrift-shop sweater that I spun clean in the dorm washing machines, while I sat on top, reading Milton and drinking a milkshake. I see myself sitting across from Nick, see my chest rise as I take a long breath. I am deliberating. I am trying to put this delicately.

"I can't."

They are the only two words that come through my memory unbroken. They are clear and harsh, even though I remember saying them softly, regretfully. I remember surrounding them with gentle reasoning and sound statements. Apologizing.

I remember being surprised at how readily and unexpectedly the words came to me. I see myself, presented with that future—the life of the missionary wife, the one I had at one time so desperately wanted. It is wrapped like a gift. I could reach out, and it would be mine—the European flat, the thick, dark coffee. Late night Bible studies and cobblestone streets and scarves. All I had to do was take it.

But unexpected things had happened in Minnesota. There had been suspicious roommates, and there had been faraway planes crashing into faraway buildings. Mostly, there had been that Moment when a missionary boy gave me That Look I'd seen so many times before, and for the first time, I wanted to run.

I want to explain this to Nick in the coffee shop when he makes his unexpected request. I want to tell him that this is not just about the heart necklace; it's about the way it had become so clear. The world had changed, and I had changed, and I did not want my life mapped out for me, tethered to the dreams of someone else. I wanted to move forward into the blank pages of my own life. I wanted to write the story myself.

But I can't find the words to tell him this, so I just say, "I can't."

And it is not a love story, and it's not a breakup story. It's a story about that shocking, fearful moment when the trajectory of your life changes. The Boy says, "Marry me," and your chest constricts and something that has always defined you breaks. And it is *freedom*.

In the coffee shop, Nick studies his hands on the table. Behind us the wind beats against the window, and I feel strong and wholly myself. The afternoon is darkening almost imperceptibly into night; the streetlights are flickering on to light the way.

—◼ ▬

When I got back to Northwestern after Christmas break, everything felt different. After all, when the tectonic plates of your life shift in such a monumental way, there is bound to be some fallout. Your perceptions of the world get covered in the grimy dust, accumulated over so many years, that now flies free around you.

In the wake of my breakthrough, I began to withdraw from the

Northwestern student culture. I stopped going to the Wednesday night student-led worship service, "The Edge," and while my dorm Bible study attendance had been sparse up until that point, it stopped altogether in January. It wasn't that I was *backsliding,* though it certainly appeared that way to my roommates who were heaving deep, agonized sighs when I left for my cold, nighttime walks with Andrew. I continued to fill prayer journals with long lines of praise and prayer. I continued to read my Bible, to let the words lift me through each day. Once a week, Kim and I drove to Panera to eat bagels and drink Dr Pepper and talk about the particulars of our spiritual lives.

But at Northwestern, I edged toward the periphery. In the mandatory morning chapel services, I moved from the center rows to the back, near the door. I sat next to Andrew, holding his hand while the dean preached on verse after verse in the book of Matthew. I leaned against his shoulder, and he put his head against mine, and I could feel his curls soft against my head.

Some mornings, we didn't go to chapel at all. We scanned our student IDs to avoid "failing to attend" fines, and we then disappeared into the mob of students, working our way to the back doors. We spent the hour sitting on a bench, not saying much of anything, just staring together out into the beautiful world.

It was in those days that a subtle change began to occur for me. As I idled in the haven of spirituality that was Northwestern, I began to quietly resent the evangelicals: the faithful ones who led Bible studies and remained at the Top of the Spectrum. The ones who seemed to be looking at me with a certain amount of wariness. I began to see them as one body, as a Force that could hurt me if I let it. I had good friends, and I gathered them around me in the cafeteria and outside on the pathways and in the moments between classes, but I never again entered the throbbing evangelical culture with the same kind of abandon.

I made a home for myself, instead, in the English department. I surrounded myself with artists and poets. They seemed softer than the oth-

ers, their spiritual fervor tempered by the power of art. I learned to read
the Bible with an eye turned to my newly forming identity. I read in the
Gospels about a woman who had been bleeding for many years. She
came to Jesus and touched His cloak in the hopes that He would heal her.
I learned that only when she turned to the crowd and told her story out
loud did He tell her to go in peace. I felt so much like that woman. I
began to tell my story in halting, simple prose and poetry.

I made a home for myself with Andrew, who seemed to live his life
on a different frequency than everyone else. If he cared what people
thought of him or his faith, he never showed it. He did not vie for positions of spiritual leadership or talk about his life's calling; instead he
played intramural basketball. I sat in the bleachers with my books and
papers and watched as he dribbled, passed, his calves going taut as he
jumped to make the shot.

He had a casual disregard for Northwestern's many Rules. It's not as
if he set out to break them; he just didn't factor them into his daily decisions. He made a habit of ditching class on Fridays, shrugging and laughing when his teachers mentioned his absence. Occasionally, he showed up
at my door when it was not visiting hours at all, and I had to rush him,
laughing, down the hall and outside before we both got fined.

He laughed, and he made me laugh, and it was because his relationship to his faith was not a do-or-die mission but something life-giving
and fluid. Like a river. Like a fountain. It was in the generosity of his faith
and his love that I found the rest I'd been hoping for when I filled out the
applications and packed my bags for Minnesota.

That January, our friends spray-painted our names on that big boulder, The Rock, in typical Northwestern College fashion. *Andrew + Addie*
it said in big pink letters. I'm sure some cynical student walked by that
day and rolled his eyes. *Another Northwestern marriage,* he thought to
himself. Only it wasn't really. It was a dialogue. It was a partnership. It
was a love story. We were just two kids from the middle of the spectrum.
No one knew us. But we knew each other. And it was enough.

— ◆ —

The last time I saw Nick, he was engaged, and so was I, our lives back in tandem as they always were. I would marry Andrew, and Nick would marry one of those punk-rock Christian girls I'd always envied. Her name was Riley, and she had that short, bleached-blond haircut that I'd always wanted to be able to pull off. Our weddings would occur within weeks of each other at the end of the summer.

Nick and I came upon each other one summer night at Vertical Impact, both of us home…both of us standing in the crowded room, trying to remember who we had once been. When we spoke, our conversation was stilted, awkward.

"Congratulations," I'd said, smiling. "She's perfect for you."

"Yeah," he said, beaming across the room at his fiancée, her short, spiked hair glinting under the lights. "She is."

"Aren't you glad I said no?" I said it quietly, and he did not respond. I don't know if he heard me or not, and I realize now that this was not the most sensitive thing to say. What I was trying to say was: *This is how it was always supposed to turn out.* What I was trying to say was that I was glad that I had known him, but that I was never meant to be his missionary wife, that we had chosen the right path, and that we'd both ended up right where we were supposed to be.

"Hey, look, I gotta go," he said. Riley was waving him over across the room. "It was nice to see you, though. I hope your wedding is amazing."

"Thanks," I said. "Yours too."

He looked at me for one more moment, and then he was gone, the last of the missionary boys, disappearing into the crowd.

Twelve

Saving Oneself for Marriage: To remain sexually abstinent until your wedding day. In the nineties, this concept became so intrinsically linked to the momentum of the evangelical youth culture that sexual purity and spiritual purity became almost synonymous for many struggling teens.

Wow," I said, pulling the flimsy negligee out of the gift bag. It was pink with black ruffles, meant to look, I guessed, like the uniform that a naughty French maid might wear.

"Woo-hoo!" my four bridesmaids hooted in tandem. It was tawdry. It was tasteless. It was, of course, from Kim and Alissa.

It was three days before my wedding, and true, I had been thinking about the sex. It had occurred to me, actually, only a couple of weeks before. I had gone to Minnesota spontaneously to see Andrew for the weekend. I was spending the summer at my parents' house back in Chicago, working at a catalog company and planning our wedding. He was assembling machinery at a small shop and spending his evenings shooting hoops in his folks' driveway.

It was July. Seeing as our wedding was so close and seeing as we'd been apart for so long, the one-kiss-per-day rule that we'd put in place during our dating days seemed, suddenly, antiquated and highly unnecessary. We walked hand in hand across his parents' farm in the still summer night, the fields bathed in moonlight, the stars hopeful and close.

We stopped to kiss. We kissed more. We kissed until it became a sort of desperation to get closer, closer, as close as possible, and we were lying down, kissing madly in the dewy midnight grass. And suddenly, I was Awake.

I rocketed away from him, scared, I think, by the very presence of it—this desire so real and tangible in that well-kept secret of my body. My sexuality stunned me as it emerged sudden and fully developed. I suppose it had always been there. I suppose it had been waiting for a moment like this, waiting for me to let my guard down enough to discover it.

It is the timing of this "awakening" that to this day surprises me and that I can only account for as a kind of grace. I was so close to my wedding day. I could wait to give in to it. The defenses I'd placed between myself and my body's most intense desires—the Rules, the dating contracts, the Christian music, the family-friendly television shows I watched—they had somehow formed a protective layer that held through high school's tumult and through my early college years and through the greater part of my engagement. It was only now, a month before our wedding day, disappearing into the vast starry night.

If this moment had occurred earlier, or if I had married later, I don't know how things would have turned out. Would my evangelical ideals about sex before marriage have held? Or would I have given in to the beauty of intimacy under some full harvest moon with some beautiful boy?

—◆—

"Fashion show! Fashion show!" Kim hollered at the bachelorette party, clapping insistently.

"Whatever," I said, blushing. "I am *not* giving you a lingerie fashion show. But thank you." I nodded toward the negligee, so foreign to me, so filmy and unfamiliar as I put it into the gift bag. "I'm sure Andrew will love this."

My little sister whistled, flipping her short red hair behind her ear.

"Well, that's okay, because it's time for Bachelorette Party: Part 2!" Alissa announced, giving Kim a meaningful look. "To the Jeep!"

"What's part two? What's part two?"

"It's a secret. You'll find out when we get there."

It, of course, wasn't the kind of scandal common to a typical bachelorette party. I was barely twenty, none of my bridesmaids quite twenty-one, my little sister still only sixteen. There would be no bars. No shots or pitchers of beer. No boys sucking Life Savers off a slutty T-shirt or grinding drunkenly with strangers on a darkened dance floor. This was not a life I had known. It was not a life I was leaving, not a life I realized I was giving up.

Instead, Bachelorette Party: Part 2 took us to one of the country's largest evangelical megachurches, Willow Creek. The church was located in one of Chicago's most affluent suburbs, and it had a parking lot that went on forever. Tonight, there were only a few lonely cars scattered haphazardly across the concrete. Wide, lit windows showed empty corridors and darkened classrooms. It was after midnight. There was no one around.

Kim cut the lights before we drove in and eased the car onto the grassy banks of the baptismal pond before putting it into Park.

"And welcome to Part 2. Skinny-dipping," Alissa announced.

"Are you kidding me?" I asked.

"Ha!" Kim laughed. "Definitely not."

We'd gone skinny-dipping once before, Kim, Alissa, and I. We'd done it on a post–high school graduation camping trip, running across the broad field of a closed state park to get to the lakeshore, hearts pounding, hitting the ground every time a car roared by. It had felt so scandalous then, so illicit, so freeing.

"In the *baptismal pond*?" Katie, my only married bridesmaid, laughed.

"Alissa, I saw you get baptized here! I saw your parents get baptized here! I can't jump into this pond naked!" I'd stood on this shore while three pastors held them simultaneously—Alissa, her mom, her dad—and then pulled them into the water in the name of the Father and the Son and the Holy Spirit.

"You can, and you will," Kim said, hopping out of her car. "You only have one bachelorette party."

"True," I said, sliding out into the quiet night. I idled for a second in the moonlight, and then shrugged. "All right. Well, here we go."

I stripped behind the car, thin and lovely and *pure* in the summer dark. My body was untouched, my virginity intact, and yet, the truth is, I had not been altogether "saved for marriage" as the old True Love Waits campaign implied I could be.

No one really is.

I had been broken, and there were all these sharp places that I couldn't see inside myself. My heart had known so much. And the man I would marry held his own deep brokenness too, his own struggles and pain. When our hearts joined in marriage, we would find ourselves bleeding inexplicably from each other's hidden edges.

But that night, I didn't understand that. As far as I knew, I had made it. I was closing in on the finish line, and my bridesmaids and I were *running*. We were ripping off our clothes and running toward the pond, leaving jeans and sandals and bras strewn haphazardly on the well-manicured grass. Then, we were in the pond, moving in slow motion, the moon igniting the water on our skin so that when I looked over at my best friends, they glowed luminous, their breasts shining atop the water as they screamed and splashed and disappeared under the surface.

Later, there would be a wedding and a hundred thousand floating bubbles as Andrew and I got into our car and drove away, my veil flapping in the wind. Later still, there would be a Wedding Night and that first beautiful, awkward foray into lovemaking in a dark hotel room in Michigan.

But for now, there was only this: the water all around me as I dove underneath the surface of the pond and came up baptized, body and spirit united for the first time in desire and in hope. My hair was floating soft, my friends were laughing above the surface. Love was all around, as clear and as bright as the moonlight.

Thirteen

Local Church: The church where you worship on Sunday mornings; the particular group of believers to whom you belong.

On Sunday mornings, Andrew and I take a rickshaw through the dusty streets of Pinghu, China, to church. The rickshaw driver is small, and his head bobs as he pedals the bicycle through the poor part of town.

The school where we teach is on the main drag of Pinghu, a street crammed with fluorescent lighting, lined with restaurants and cell phone stores and the town Century Mart. But the road to church is muted, and the shops have an empty, frugal feel to them. They are the size, roughly, of American one-car garages; their proprietors are stirring large pots of noodles or are sitting, feet up, behind crates of earth-caked vegetables. Children play in the dusty street and wave to us when we go by.

The rickshaw drops us at the gate to the Chinese Three Self Church, the only State-sanctioned Protestant church in Pinghu. We walk through an archway into an open-air courtyard where small, wrinkled church women move smoothly around us, offering delicate Chinese hellos. *Ni hao.*

There are fourteen of us. Fourteen American English teachers living in Pinghu, a rural town of half a million, nestled among the rice paddies that stretch south from Shanghai. We do not meet in the main sanctuary of the church with the Chinese worshipers. We meet instead in the upper room of a small building next door. The purpose, after all, of a government-sanctioned church is to remove foreign influence from

Chinese worship and to ensure devotion to the People's Republic of China. So we become an ornament, decorative and off to the side.

— —

Andrew and I arrived in China through a series of murky connections: a college professor knew a guy who knew a guy who put us in touch with F. S. Zhang, the current president of Shin Sheng High School in Pinghu. Andrew had been hoping for placement within a Chinese business to give him the foreign experience required to complete his international business degree, but there was nothing. Just this. Just F. S. Zhang and his school full of Chinese students in Pinghu. Not ideal—but good enough to satisfy the school requirement. We signed a contract, committing to teach English there for one year.

The rest of the American English teachers here knew one another before they came. They were graduates of an ultraconservative college in Michigan, where they had lived in close quarters for the past four years. This college, we learned, was fed by the homeschooled children of an older generation of fundamentalist Christians. They came from families of twelve, thirteen, fourteen—families who did not believe birth control to be part of God's plan, families who sent their children to the College in Michigan, a steady dripping, one after another, until the school became a sort of giant, extended family.

I had never seen anything like them: this group of college grads moved in the halting, awkward manner of people still controlled—some willingly, some less so—but all of them still held hostage by the school they came from, the school that sent them here, the College in Michigan, seven thousand miles away. There were rules that made my fussy evangelical upbringing seem wild: No listening to music with drums. No movies with a rating exceeding PG. No public displays of affection.

But the most bizarre of the school-enforced restrictions was that which addressed the issue of wardrobe. The women were to wear skirts or dresses at all times—knee-length, minimum. Pinghu sweltered in the summer. The dishrag sky would wring itself over the town, leaving everything streaked gray, plastering the long skirts against the legs of the Michigan girls as they walked from class to class. Then, in the winter, the icy winds came, making the long hours of teaching in unheated classrooms unbearable. The girls took to wearing layers of tights and pants underneath their skirts to ward off the cold. The skirts lay awkwardly over the layers, puffy and cumbersome, someone's misconstrued version of modesty. Constantly getting in the way.

—   —

The ritual rickshaw ride to church in the morning feels preposterous to me right from the start. After all, we live on the same campus, all of us just one floor apart in the teachers' dormitory. Across the courtyard, the boys' building stands six floors high, and at night, the students walk up and down the outdoor corridors in their underwear, washing their clothes in plastic buckets and hanging them to dry. When they see us out, they wave and holler, "Hello, teacher!"

Andrew and I had been married for a year by the time we got to China. We married the summer before our senior year in a wedding filled with envious college friends and pink roses and prayer. We spent our last year at Northwestern living in Married Student Housing, where we were constantly throwing parties with frozen pizzas and bags of chips, which I liked to pour into the colorful serving bowls that I'd gotten at our wedding. We were away from the main campus, inaccessible to the roving RAs. We were a safe place. We were a gathering place.

There was no alcohol at those parties, but there wasn't really a need for any. We were *that* happy. That complete. We crammed into our tiny living room, overflowed into the kitchen. We played cards on the garage sale kitchen table and video games on the used Nintendo system, and in the early morning, when the last guests disappeared out of the sliding glass door, Andrew and I fell asleep easily to the steady flow of cars as they passed by on Snelling Avenue.

We didn't go to a local church during that year. Our church was all around us, eating stale sandwiches in the booths of the college cafeteria, sitting side by side in classes. In getting married, we had escaped dorm life and were free to surround ourselves with our closest college friends, the ones we'd gathered along the way. That was our sweetest year.

And now, here we were again, surrounded by evangelicals. Sort of.

"Why don't we just do church at our apartment on Sunday mornings?" Andrew suggested at the beginning of our time in China. He brought it up to the Leader of the Homeschoolers, Mark. He was a kind of emissary for the College in Michigan. Though he was their peer, barely twenty himself, it fell to him to enforce the rules, to make sure the girls kept wearing those long skirts, to raise an eyebrow pointedly if hemlines seemed too short.

"We can have coffee, and Addie can make cinnamon rolls or something," Andrew continued. "We can share what we're learning and do some worship songs and make it kind of low-key."

"No," Mark said, closing his brown eyes and sighing through his nose. He had a long, slow voice and a lot of product in his black hair keeping it slicked into place. He said his words very deliberately, staring at us as he spoke. "We need to go to church."

"But we *are* The Church," Andrew said. This is one of his favorite biblical truths, this idea of church as a moveable feast, an ever-present community—church not as a *place* you go to, with walls and crosses and long rows of pews, but as something that happens spontaneously when two or three Christians are gathered together in one location. To Andrew, it meant that everything we do is worship, that Sunday morning is just another time, another place. Not *The* Time. Not *The* Place.

But Mark did not see it that way. To Mark, the Leader of the Homeschoolers, church was very much a place, and it was located on the other end of Pinghu. There were people expecting to see us there, and we would not disappoint.

"Yes," Mark conceded, "but we still need to *go* to church."

"Right," Andrew had said. "Okay." Even though it wasn't, really.

So on Sunday mornings, Andrew and I hold hands in the rickshaw as we ride through the dusty morning streets of Pinghu. We sit at repurposed school desks in the upstairs of the Three Self Church and stare ahead at long red curtains framing a white cross. The entire room smells of chalk and sweat. *Sanctuary.* We are silenced by some invisible weight, the layers of decorum lying awkwardly over us, making us move in stunted ways. "Good morning," we say to one another as we take our seats and wait for the service to begin.

—•—

Church worship is led by Courtney, a former music major from the College in Michigan, who brings her violin and saws out melodies while the rest of us sing tentatively along. When her fingers climb over the E string and the notes get high, we all struggle to find the coordinating low note. The result is a sort of uncomfortable dissonance, our voices reaching awkwardly toward heaven and coming up short.

We stand at the desks. It is customary in an evangelical church service to stand during worship, and we are doing things the customary way. Mark has arranged these services so that they mirror those we have left behind in America, the services whose structures and traditions stay with us, a phantom limb. *Enter. Wait. Sing. Pray. Listen. Sing. Pray.* It's the same every week.

One Sunday, F. S. Zhang attends our service. He sits at a desk on the left side of the room, his arms folded across his customary short-sleeved polo as we stand to sing. Courtney calls out a hymn number, and Andrew holds out the song book so I can see the words and follow along the bars of music.

"It Is Well with My Soul" is one of my favorite hymns of all time. It was written by Horatio Spafford, a man ruined by the Great Chicago Fire. With all his possessions burned away, he had sent his wife and daughters ahead to Europe by ship to start a new life, planning to follow them once he'd gotten things in order in Chicago. But there was a collision in transit. He received the telegram from his wife while he was still in Chicago, picking up the pieces of their lives in the ashes. "Saved alone," the telegram had said.

"When peace like a river attendeth my way, when sorrows like sea billows roll…" He had penned it somewhere in the middle of that great, expansive ocean, the story goes, after a crew member pointed out to him where his daughters' ship had gone down. "Whatever my lot, Thou hast taught me to say, It is well, it is well with my soul." I imagined him singing those words, his eyes stinging with sadness and salt, and yet clinging to a loving God somewhere, everywhere, invisible but *there,* near to him in the silent sky.

"We'll sing the first, third, and final verses," Courtney says loudly, and then she begins playing, the melody harsh in the morning quiet. We sing along as best we can, Andrew next to me pausing and then starting up again, trying to find low enough notes to accommodate his voice.

And my favorite hymn in the upper room in China sounds nothing like my favorite hymn. There is a formality about it that I believe Horatio Spafford could never have intended as he sang the lyrics the first time on that sad ocean voyage.

When we finish, Mr. Zhang walks up to the front of the room. He peers over his glasses at us, and then he begins to speak in halting English.

"You sing only a few verse," he says, crossing his arms. "This no good. You must sing *all* verses. We do again."

Courtney blinks a couple of times, surprised. Andrew and I look quickly at each other, and I see him briefly close his eyes. I know what he is thinking, because it is the same thing I am thinking. We should be sprawled across the furniture in our apartment. We should have warm mugs of coffee in our hands and cinnamon rolls. This should all look different.

But Mr. Zhang has taken his seat and is waiting, arms crossed, for us to oblige, and we feel the weight of his expectation, his dark eyes fixing us in place. We are suspended in the upper room by Mark and by the others—the only Americans here in this town—and by the sanctuary full of Chinese congregants below. And we want to leave, but we can't seem to make our legs walk away from it.

Courtney lifts her violin back to her shoulder, and we shuffle back to standing. Andrew picks the hymnal up and leafs noisily through to do it all over again.

— ■ ■ —

Someone has brought a pulpit to the upper room for us, and the men have a sign-up sheet. They each take a week or two to preach. No one asked if any of the women would like to sign up. In the world of conservative evangelical theology, women are not allowed to preach, to have "dominion over men." It is one of those "hot topics," the kind that led to raised voices and red faces at Northwestern College. I gathered from the quiet, unquestioning acceptance from the Michigan girls that it hadn't even been a discussion for them.

I don't think it occurred to me then to be outraged by this, even to notice it as it happened. Week after week, the men got up and spoke on some scripture. I don't remember much of what they said. Most Sundays I stared out the window and thought of home.

If I could have preached, I think I may have talked about the Israelites as they fled the tyranny of the Egyptians, as they left behind their life of slavery and set off toward the Promised Land with Moses. I would have read the passages where they complain because they are hungry.

Usually, when pastors read this passage, they berate the Israelites for their lack of faith. "They had just seen God part the Red Sea," the pastors say. "They walked between two *walls of water*. And then, *days later*, they're whining! They're asking to go back!"

And there was a time when this rendering made sense to me. There was a time when it spurred me to grasp harder to my faith, to hang on with white knuckles to the promises of God while the world shifted around me.

But here in China, I am experiencing a depth of hunger I have not known before. We are existing on cold blocks of rice from the cafeteria, on slimy chunks of tofu and on fish that still have all of their scales and both of their eyes. On our nights off, we are eating in small local restaurants that lace their noodles with handfuls of MSG. We are ordering unfamiliar food from menus by pointing at the photographs.

I don't belong here. I miss cheese. I miss spaghetti and chicken breasts and Kraft Macaroni & Cheese with its familiar orange cheese-dust. I have begun, already, to stockpile rolls of Oreo and Chips Ahoy! cookies in our small apartment. Pringles. M&M'S. DoveBars—the American snack foods I can find in the local Chinese markets. I eat them with a kind of desperation. A need for the familiar. I am gaining weight; I am losing color.

I am not a missionary wife. Andrew's Chinese classes had always been for business, not for the express purpose of translating Bibles or witnessing to unreached cities, and I took comfort in that during our college days. He'd never spoken of having a "heart" for China the way missionary boys did. Andrew had a heart for *God*, a generous orthodoxy that allowed him to go anywhere, be anything. His daily tasks reverberated with love; everything mattered.

I'm not a missionary wife, but at the same time, I live in Pinghu, China. I eat blocks of cold tofu. It's as if I'm a missionary wife.

I am crippled by my lack of knowledge, my lack of language. The only place I can go by myself is the market, where I know how to read the total off the cash register and count out my Chinese yuan. I can't explain to the postal clerks that I want to send a package to America. I cannot explain to the clothing merchants that I want to try on a dress. I miss saying, "How are you doing today?" I miss having people smile and say it back to me.

And I feel for the Israelites, far from all they knew, hungry for familiarity. I am beginning to think a miracle is an awfully evasive thing. I am beginning to think the memory of even the most extraordinary act of God can so easily slip away in those moments of your endless hunger.

And sitting in the upper room of that church in China, I begin to wonder about it all for the first time—the voices of women, their role in church life. It occurs to me later that if I had been able to voice my hunger, maybe it would have been like a bridge that connected the need in me to the need in them, the Michigan girls. Maybe if I'd been able to stand up and talk about the darkness, it would not have consumed me.

— ▪ —

Our little group of foreign English teachers learns to rely on one another in certain ways. We cover each other's classes when conflicts arise; we share lesson plans; after midterms, we sit together at a large conference table, grading tall stacks of exam booklets.

On Sunday nights, everyone crams into our apartment to watch two or three episodes of *Alias* on DVD, a spy drama that Mark has grudgingly approved. They come in one by one with their pillows and pile on the hard tile floor of our living room. When they leave, the place is strewn with wrappers and empty Pepsi bottles. When it's time to celebrate a birthday, we all chip in to buy a cake and a gift. The candle plays a loop of birthday music and blazes like a sparkler, and to get it to stop singing, someone stomps on it until the sound cuts out and the burnt wick crumbles on the floor.

It's a good thing we have going. Not quite *friendship*, but a kind of piecemeal family. We are together in Pinghu, the only Americans for miles and miles. We make the best of it.

The problem is I need more.

I need a best friend. Or two. Or three. I need Kim and Alissa, the girls who know me best, know me longest. I need to be able to flop down on someone's bed and bury my head in her pillow and cry until I'm all out of tears because I'm homesick and I'm tired and the gray of Pinghu is smothering me.

I need *real* fellowship, the kind that goes deeper than lesson plans and church foyer talk. But I can't figure out how to get there. The Michigan girls elude me, their friendship tight-sealed together over so many years. I can feel myself shrinking inward, withdrawing, but I feel powerless to change it. Instead, I watch pirated *Friends* DVDs that I bought one date night in Jiaxing. I start at Season 1 and watch until the very end. And then I start over.

— ◆ —

On our first school holiday, our entire team takes a trip up to Beijing. We ride a train overnight, sleeping on bunks that tower three high and shake as the train rushes north over the expansive Chinese landscape. It is fall, but so far, it has not felt that way in Pinghu. Summer has stretched into September and October. Where I'd been expecting a crisp freshness, there has only been the same bulky humidity that settled over my shoulders on the first day here. But when we step off the train in Beijing, it is orange and red and yellow. Fall.

We eat that first lunch at a Pizza Hut, which is laid out exactly as it is at home, the same booths, the same hanging lights. I think about how *colorful* it feels inside the Pizza Hut. I cut my slice of pan-style pepperoni into small bites and feel deeply grateful each time I raise my fork to my mouth.

In Beijing, Andrew and I split off from the group and go to the International Church, a service held in the heart of the city for expats and English teachers and all manner of ragged Western strangers.

Around us, English speakers file in. We can hear them laughing American laughs. We can hear snatches of conversation rise and fall in familiar syntax—level English words that do not require the impossible-to-master tones of Chinese.

In the moments before the service begins, the couple in front of us turns around to say hello. The man is from Minnesota. *Minnesota!* He says the names of familiar suburbs—Maple Grove, Roseville, Plymouth—and he speaks in elongated *o*'s, the accent of home. His dark-haired wife smiles sweetly at us.

The music starts playing. Guitars. They are strumming softly, and there are people on stage singing, and it is a kind of comfort. The sound is holding me, and I am clinging to it, and I am crying, softly at first, but it deepens into a kind of uncontrollable sadness. Andrew puts his arm around me, and it is strong. His voice is steady as he sings quietly, holding me. The dark-haired woman in front of us rummages in her purse for a tissue and then turns to hand it to me.

I am crying because there is a kind of beauty to all of it, as though God is here. I can almost see Him. I can *almost see Him,* and it's been months since I've felt this close to the Divine. It's as if the smog has created a sort of impenetrable shield over Pinghu, and our awkward worship can't pierce it, and the boys' hastily written sermons can't pierce it, and the pages and pages of frantic cursive in my prayer journal can't pierce it. It's as if God can't get to me. Or won't.

Andrew rubs my shoulder as I stand next to him in pieces. He knows I am struggling to find my way in China, but he is one of the chameleon people, completely adaptable, at ease in so many different places and circumstances. So much of him thrives on this, the adventure of it, the unknown of it. At night, he likes us to go out into the town, to walk among the vendors, through the open market where local farmers are selling vegetables alongside pails of live snakes, eels, turtles. When we sit at a restaurant eating, he cocks his ear and tries to piece the Chinese words together and translate it into conversation.

But the longer we stay here, the more I feel myself disappearing. I need God to reach out of the sky and grab hold of me with one big, invisible hand. It needs to happen now, before I lose myself in this sadness.

fourteen

Church Shopping/Hunting: The process of visiting a
number of churches, looking for the one you will commit
to attending.

We get home from China on the Fourth of July. We celebrate with
gusto, eating hot dogs from a vendor and watching a Little
League game, and we are wildly glad to be American when the fireworks
shoot bright across the sky.

We celebrate and we visit friends and family, and then we set about
the work of starting a new life.

We move into an apartment in Plymouth, a suburb of Minneapolis
just a fifteen-minute dash from the heart of the city. Andrew hangs his
souvenir Chinese swords on the walls, and I unpack my dishes and my
cookie cutters and my picture frames, holding them gratefully in my
hands before I set them up. I have a brand-new job across the city, writing
manuals at a software development company; Andrew sells ID printers
from a small office in Eden Prairie.

I am beginning to slowly shake off the gray of Pinghu. I take deep
breaths of the air, and it smells like home. In these early days I go to Target, just to stand there, to feel the pulsing of my familiar culture as it
surges around me. Busy people go about their distinctly American er-
rands, and I am happy just to be among them again. When people ask
me about the trip, I say things like, "It was interesting," and "It was a
challenge. Hard. But good." But the reality is, I am trying to purge my
system of the whole dark thing. It is poetic, really, that every morning I

have to take a handful of herbal pills to systematically kill off the parasite that found its way into my stomach in China. I swallow the pills with my breakfast, every morning checking the bottle to see how many are left, how much closer I am to the cure.

I waste no time setting us on a traditional, evangelical church-shopping excursion. I am aware of how distant God feels, how far away I feel from myself. And somewhere in my earliest memories, the Church People are smiling down at me, holding me close. I was born into them, these evangelical Church People. They were my home…and here, at twenty-two, I am desperately homesick.

Andrew still finds church buildings themselves to be a bit suspect. He'd prefer a house church, a living room gathering. But those are hard to find. I search the Internet and create a masterful spreadsheet: a row for each local church, columns for ministries, location, pros and cons. I hand it to him one night while we eat dinner on our threadbare hand-me-down couch and watch *Wheel of Fortune.*

Andrew glances at the spreadsheet, and somehow he sees the truth behind it—my need, my unspoken struggle. "These look good," he says, glancing at the names. "Which one do you want to try first?" I smile and rest against his shoulder. "Doesn't matter," I tell him, even though it does. Even though I know so much hinges on the right church.

We begin to hunt.

It is tedious and difficult, this search for a group of Christians that will become *your* Christians, your church family. It's this step that so often trips people up. There are so many churches. They rise up from so many corners, from strip malls, from great fields that would be empty but for the big new building and its glassy black parking lot. *So many* churches, but also, never the one you're looking for. Never the church you have in your head, the one you went to when you were a kid, where everyone knew your name, where you fit like a puzzle piece.

Sometimes, many times, they stop looking, the evangelical post-grads. On Sunday morning, they wake and think, *Let's just skip it this morning.* They don't intend to abandon their church hunt; it just kind of happens.

But I am desperate in a way that even I can't understand. So every Sunday, Andrew and I pull ourselves out of bed early enough to make it to the late service of one of the churches on my list.

We know how it goes. We know the general layout of church foyers and where the giant silver vats of coffee can be found. If the church serves complimentary donuts with the coffee, it is duly noted in the "pros" column. Each Sunday, Andrew and I navigate the clusters of suburban Church People to the Welcome Center to get an information packet.

We stand with the congregation for worship. We try to get the feel of the music style. We are directed to turn and greet the people sitting around us, so for an awkward moment, we turn, looking for empty hands to grasp. "Hello," we say. "Good morning," they say back.

When the pastor begins his sermon, I page through the church bulletin, trying to get a sense of the church's ministries. The flow of its resources and attention. I am looking, specifically, for what they have to offer us: married, in our early twenties, without kids. I am looking for a kind of instant community. A kind of magic. I am looking for Our People—the ones who will become our dearest friends. The ones who will *get* us immediately the second we meet.

If there is communion, we take it. If the silver plate comes to collect the morning offering, we pass it on without putting money inside.

On our way out, we move slowly through the foyer, making lots of eye contact. We are hoping someone notices that we're new, that we're looking for any reason to stay and talk. Maybe it is unfair to expect this, but I can't help but think that if two junior high girls could handle this on my first day of youth group, certainly these Church People can too.

But for the most part, no one ever stops us. We slip out of these nondescript evangelical churches generally unnoticed; we never go back.

In the end, we choose Edgebrook Evangelical Free Church not because it is a superb church, but because on our first visit there, someone finally *sees* us.

Edgebrook is a sprawling white church that straddles two affluent suburbs, pulling into its fold smartly dressed couples with smartly dressed children. When we walk in on that first Sunday, a woman with three such children notices us wandering through the hallways in search of the sanctuary. "Welcome!" she says warmly, and in spite of ourselves, we feel welcome. "Let me introduce you to our new adult ministries pastor, Carl. You'll just *love* him."

She leads us through the Sunday crowds, and she chats idly with us about where we live and what brought us to Edgebrook Free. We are in front of the sanctuary when we finally come upon him, a short man with a patchy goatee. The friendly Church Mom beams up at him. "Pastor Carl! I'd love you to meet Andrew and…" She turns to me briefly, asking, "What was your name again?"

I tell her quickly, offering a tentative smile to both of them.

"Andrew and Addie," she finishes. "Pastor Carl and his family just moved here from China."

"Really?" Andrew says. "We were just in China too."

And off they go, calculating the distance between the Chinese province where they lived and the one where we lived, trading summarized experiences with a kind of surprised relief.

"Yes," Pastor Carl says eventually, "it was very hard to leave. China was our home, and we have such a heart for the Chinese people." He looks wistfully through the crowds of people moving toward the sanctuary. The music is beginning, and guys with guitars on stage are playing an upbeat worship song. A few people are clapping.

He shakes himself out of his nostalgia. "But we know God has called us here for a reason, and I'm so glad to meet you guys. You'll have to check out our Young Adult group next week. It meets during the nine o'clock service."

"Seems nice," Andrew whispers a few minutes later, as we take our seats.

"Nice," I echo, smiling at him. And he was, of course, this Chinese missionary pastor. There is no reason for the apprehension I feel sinking over me. I know that the trapped feeling has less to do with Pastor Carl than it does with the sudden mention of China.

I focus on the people around me, on the American voices, on the Minnesotan *o*'s as they greet one another. The gray-haired lead pastor has clearly just learned to use PowerPoint, and free Internet clip art keeps flying dramatically onto the screen. *It's okay,* I tell myself. *China is over. We're home. We're home. We're home.*

— —

The Young Adults class meets in a long classroom next to the sanctuary, and when we gather there in the morning, we can hear the music from the nine o'clock church service next door pressing up against the thin walls.

Scattered among the rows of folding chairs, couples speak in whispers until class starts. It is odd and quiet. There is a table with coffee and donuts in the corner of the room, but no one clusters around it chatting. It's as though they have worked out some sort of complicated choreography so that they're never caught in awkward conversation. I can tell immediately that this is not the magic community I'd been hoping for. These are not our kind of people at all.

But we give it a try anyway. You can only church hunt for so long before you either have to give up or just settle in somewhere and see how it goes. We are settling in, somewhat uncomfortably, in a row of folding chairs. We are trying to make eye contact with the other couples. I notice that many of the women are wearing long skirts and ironed blouses, and I have a sudden, gripping flashback to the upper room in Pinghu, China. I am, as usual, wearing jeans.

Pastor Carl teaches briefly and then splits us up into groups for discussion, handing us all photocopied lists of questions. Andrew always goes off-book, tossing the discussion guide to the side before he even looks at it.

When we pull our chairs across the carpet to sit across from a young, good-postured couple, Andrew immediately flashes a dimpled smile. "Hey there," he says, and I love him for his genuine kindness and his easy smile. He reaches to shake the man's hand and then the woman's. The man opens his mouth to talk, but his wife is already going.

"I'm Anna. This is Paul."

"Great to meet you guys," Andrew says, and he means it. His sincerity somehow puts everyone at ease, including me, sitting much too close to the good-postured Anna, trying not to pick at a renegade thread that is coming loose at the knee of my jeans.

Anna is a talker, and Paul lets her go. Andrew only has to ask her a few leading questions to learn that she is a pharmacist's assistant and Paul is a software developer and they live in Plymouth and have been coming to this church for nine or ten months. Paul splits his gaze between the bottoms of his khaki pants and the animated face of his wife. He has glasses that are too big for his face, and his hair is gelled at the part.

We learn that they met on a two-week mission trip, and I immediately feel defensive and irritable. "It was the Lord," she says sweetly, and Paul smiles at her. And I think, yes, it was probably the Lord. But also it was probably the fact that Anna is a talker and Paul is quiet. I can see them there, in Mexico, building homes for the poverty stricken. I can imagine them meeting in that alternate universe of missions work, the pressures of daily life stripped down to the simple pounding of hammer against wall. I imagine she was playing with the children; I imagine him thinking, *It might be nice to have children someday.*

Pastor Carl says, "Five minutes, guys. Wrap it up," and I realize Andrew has smoothly bypassed the sheet of discussion questions and moved instead into the conversation of daily life, the stuff that builds friendships. Anna realizes this at the same time, but she does not seem happy. "Oh my gosh," she says, glancing at the paper on the chair next to Andrew. "We didn't answer *any* of these."

"That's okay," Andrew says easily. "Why don't we just do prayer requests? That's the last thing on the list." He reads aloud, for Anna's benefit, "Share with your group one thing you'd like prayer for over the next week."

"Well," Anna says immediately, brushing her short hair back unnecessarily. "We really feel like God is calling us to the mission field full-time, and we're trying to figure out what the next step is."

I feel my eyebrows raise and quickly lower them, hoping she didn't notice.

Anna presses on. "It's just that for most of the applications for missions organizations, you need a reference from your current employer." She glances, troubled, at Paul, who is looking at the bottom of his pants again. "But if we do that, we'd be tipping them off that we're leaving."

Andrew nods, listening carefully to Anna as she goes on, but I am staring at Paul. I think, *I wonder if she realizes that she's married to a software engineer.* Paul is nodding, but he's still looking down, and no matter how hard I try, I cannot picture Paul actually wanting this missionary life.

It's a snap judgment, really. But I can't help thinking about Chris Jacobson and the way things get blurry in the presence of evangelical charisma. The way things get when you're in love. I wonder if Paul has convinced himself that he wants this life that Anna is proposing...because he wants *her*. Loves *her*. I think about the gray of China that I can't seem to shake, and I wonder if he's really ready for what's ahead.

"So"—she takes a deep breath, ready to summarize—"just pray that we would know if we should be giving our notice or what. I mean, maybe we should. Maybe we should just give our notice and trust God."

Andrew looks as if he wants to say something but then changes his mind. "Well, we'll definitely be praying for you guys."

Paul looks up slowly and gives us an unsure smile. "Thanks," he says quietly.

— • —

They hired Pastor Carl, I imagine, because he is enthusiastic, because his passion for the Lord had led him around the globe and back. They hired him to revive their dying young adult ministry, recognizing that without the involvement of the next generation of young adults, their church would not survive.

So Pastor Carl came with his three little girls and his blond, frizzy-haired wife. He is the newest staff member at Edgebrook, and he enjoys a certain amount of celebrity. When people speak of him in the fellowship hall over cups of coffee, it is with a sort of hushed reverence.

I am the exception. Something about Carl and his goatee rubs me wrong.

I figure it out on the day Pastor Carl goes on the local news to describe a study he is starting at Edgebrook Evangelical Free Church: Breaking the Da Vinci Code. The controversial movie has just hit theaters, causing uproar from evangelicals around the country. Books keep popping up in Christian bookstores, bearing strikingly similar titles. *Breaking the Da Vinci Code. Cracking Da Vinci's Code. The Da Vinci Code Mysteries. The Da Vinci Code Controversy.*

"We want to encourage people in the community to come with their questions about this movie. Together we can explore the truth about Jesus."

He flashes a smile and looks sincerely into the camera.

"Ugh," I say to Andrew, who is sitting beside me in our tiny apartment living room. "Do you think he's even read the book?"

"Probably not." Andrew shrugs, still staring at the TV. It doesn't seem to bother him.

It's not really fair for me to say it like this, because *I* haven't read the book. But Andrew has, and he was not all that scandalized by the plot. "Well, *clearly* it's not true," he'd said when I'd asked him about it. "It's a novel. It's fiction."

It's the knee-jerk reaction of the evangelicals that gets me. In one swift motion, an entire faith community has moved into a defensive pose, as if to say, "I dare you to challenge me on this, the core of my faith." It almost feels like a taunt.

It doesn't feel like an invitation, this message from Pastor Carl. It feels weak and desperate and fearful.

"Pray that our Da Vinci Code sessions would bring in a big group from the community," Pastor Carl says to us that Sunday at church.

I look down as if I am praying, but I don't pray. I just can't.

— —

There is no Edgebrook small group for women like me, just a group for women with preschoolers that is held on Wednesday mornings. There is no actual admission that women like this even exist—who are not moms but just *women*—and I know it's not personal, but it *feels* personal.

I could muster myself up and try to do something about it. I could start the group myself and fill that gaping void, but the thought makes me tired and sad.

So instead, I hang out with Gillian. She is the only single girl in the Young Adults class, heavyset with dark hair, designer glasses, and a sense of humor that dances the murky edge between funny and sinister.

A couple of Sundays ago, we both let out a kind of muffled snort when Pastor Carl mentioned, yet again, the Da Vinci Code Bible study and reminded us to invite friends. It was a friendship born of necessity, of whispered comments over the backs of the folding chairs in Sunday school. Each whispered criticism grew stronger than the last, spiraling downward into the cynical dark.

I suppose it was the way we knew how to cope. What Gillian and I had in common was this: we both felt ourselves drifting farther from the well-established center of the group, the church, evangelicalism as a whole. We were desperately wanting—*needing*—to hold on to our faith, which is why we were even *at* Edgebrook in the first place. We were homesick for something we could not name, but we were slipping. The structure of the evangelical church service was not big enough to accommodate the deep questions of our hearts.

We can't articulate any of that yet, though. All we know in those dark winter days is that if Pastor Carol mentions *The Da Vinci Code* one more time, we're both going to lose it.

We go to an Irish pub. It is the ultimate anti–small group, the two of us sitting there, gossiping about the Church People over our chicken spinach sandwiches. Gillian holds her beer stein expertly while I sip at a glass of Diet Coke. She spent her college years traipsing across Europe and feels at home in places like these. She also feels at home in the language of anger and of sadness, the irrational flinging of curse words, the pounding of her glass of beer on the table.

"I mean, who the fuck does he think he is?" Gillian says. She's talking about Pastor Carl, and I flinch a little at the word *fuck*. "He definitely has this idea of who he wants in his Young Adult group or whatever…and it's not me." Her glass thumps down between us. Amber beer sloshes over the top and runs onto the tabletop.

"Yeah…," I say, a little unsure. I take a bite of my chicken and spinach sandwich so I don't have to say more.

"I mean, no offense to you, of course," Gillian corrects herself, her eyes flitting to my wedding band. "It's not, like, your fault or anything. It's just like…he's looking for trophies or something. And you guys were in China, just like him…"

I nod, feeling the edge of her cynicism, not realizing that it is about to become my home. I'm frustrated, but I still feel a sort of muted hope. Gillian, on the other hand, is tired of trying. Of walking into that Sunday school class and feeling unwanted. She never says it in so many words, but you can tell by the way she handles her glass.

And in a way, she's right. Pastor Carl looks at us with appraising eyes when we come to class. He assumed early on that Andrew was a missionary to China, and that I was a missionary wife, when it's not true. We tried to carry the Light within us, to let it be invisible and undeniable all at once. We didn't subversively whisper the gospel, but we tried to learn our students' names. We tried to teach well. At Christmas, I drew Luke's gospel on the blackboard of my classroom. It was a diagram of stick figures: Mary, angels, shepherds orbiting around the manger like planets. I tried to speak words of Truth, but the cold was seeping into Pinghu and into my soul, and the light inside of me was flickering out.

"Yeah," I say finally. "It's ridiculous."

"I get so fucking sick of evangelicals being all starry-eyed about missionaries," Gillian says. She spits out the sentiment angrily. Also she spits out some bits of her sandwich without realizing it, and they glint green on the table. "They seriously act like that's the only way you can really be a Christian. Like we should all just pick up our bags and head over to Africa or whatever. Teach them how to live like us."

"I know," I say again, feeling a little angry myself. In my mind I can see them: the string of missionary boys from my past, marching away from me, toward some Other Place. I can still see the last of them looking over his shoulder at me, my feet planted firmly on American soil.

"Total shit," she sighs.

"*Total* shit," I agree, and the word sounds right in my mouth. Gillian laughs a little and takes another swig of her beer. We are feeling righteous in our cynicism. We are feeling wronged. We feel unarguably *right* about it.

We go on like this for another couple of weeks until Andrew and I start sleeping in on Sunday mornings. We never talk about leaving Edgebrook. We just stop getting up for it. When the alarm goes off on those Sunday mornings, we roll into each other's arms, or we drive to the Sunday morning flea market to root aimlessly through the junk of so many vendors. It just seems easier.

I lose touch with Gillian almost immediately. Our friendship, after all, was propelled by the reaction of my anger against hers, hers against mine. It was based on our common enemy. Without it, we have nothing much to say to each other.

— —

That spring, Andrew and I hear about a house church from a friend who doesn't live close enough to attend. She gives it to us like a gift.

The house church model has always appealed to us: organic and basic, a returning to those early days when disciples met in a room somewhere and broke bread.

Soon we are meeting with Bill and Sheila, the house church pastor and his wife, at the Caribou Coffee up the road. It is a Saturday morning; the light streams in through the windows and makes the red wood of the tables and walls and floors glow. People move in and out, busy and smiling, and the espresso machine grinds in the background. I can tell Andrew is electric with excitement, and I, too, feel buoyed by hope in this moment. It feels as if we have found *It* at last.

Bill and Sheila sit across from us in a sunbeam. They are middle-aged, the kind of couple who have been together long enough to start to resemble each other. They speak magic words. Words about a church where *relationships* are the thing, where discussion is valued, a church that works through the community around it, unhindered by the walls of a building, but free to move and gather and be.

"Sign us up," we say. They laugh. Bill unconsciously strokes his graying beard. This is their dream; this is the calling they feel God has placed over their lives. In a moment of generosity, they lift up the edges and let us in.

— —

We begin attending the house church in the summer. The location of our Sunday night service changes frequently, but most memorably, we meet in Bill and Sheila's small rambler in St. Louis Park. The kitchen is a flurry of noise and bodies, and there is the smell of freshly baked chocolate chip cookies. We are ushered in, and we're swept into the rhythm of their assembled church family. When we bump into someone trying to get salad, there is laughter, followed by idle, comfortable chitchat. It seems to me in retrospect that in those summer days, everyone was always smiling.

The church service is held informally as we all sit on the back porch, our plates still in front of us, still sporting the remains of our potluck dinner: a few colored rotini noodles from the pasta salad, a small dollop of unfinished spinach dip, a chicken leg sloppily eaten.

Two of the men pull out guitars as the sky begins to deepen into sunset. They strum familiar worship songs, their fingers expertly navigating the strings, matching the music with the group's voices. The music slows and then crescendos, rises up from the table and toward the purpling sky. *Bridge. Chorus. Verse. Chorus. Chorus.*

I sit in my lawn chair with my legs pulled up to my chest. I feel tears dripping onto my cheeks, but I don't feel the need to look around to see if anyone notices or if anyone cares. We are family now; we are together, lifting our voices to the heavens. The people around me are bleary and beautiful. They could be anybody. They could even be the people I want them to be.

— —

Our house church has a congregation of twenty. A few more if you include the children. The blurry, glad, getting-to-know you stage ends. The leaves begin to fall, and the congregation members come into sharp focus, their imperfections distinct and obvious.

There is, for instance, the woman with the German accent who has a lot of anecdotes about her ferrets. She says what she thinks, not bothering much with tact. One day, I confess that I've been struggling to find balance since grad school classes started. She crosses her arms and says, "It sounds like your school is interfering with your relationship with God."

The German accent gives her voice a gruffness that she probably does not intend, and I am stunned to silence.

There is the older, empty-nest couple with the matching Harleys, Tom and Janet. Although they're both nice enough, I can't get over the way Janet hardly ever smiles. She leads our impromptu worship sessions, and she's always saying things like, "Let's all stand up for the Lord!" Across the room from me, she seems formidable, lofty in her holiness. She is swaying, saying, "YES, JESUS. YES, OH LORD, WE LOVE YOU AND WANT TO DO YOUR WILL." She worships in all capitals. She murmurs. She tries to bring all of us with her. At the end of our worship times, Janet looks around, disappointed, and says, "I just don't feel like everyone was entering into the spirit of worship tonight."

The house church is full of nice young couples and nice young singles, but their politeness has a sort of empty quality to it, a hollowness that echoes in their words. And once I decide I don't fit, nothing I do seems to reverse that self-fulfilling prophecy. Once I'm aware of their faults, I can see nothing else, and I hang on to slights—real or imagined—with a firm grip. I want to let go, but I can't stop seeing them for who I wish they were. For who they're not.

I attend the women's Bible study faithfully every week, but I can't seem to wedge myself in. Each day I get a little more cynical. On Sunday nights, the young mothers talk about their children and I stand there, nodding politely, holding my plate of chicken salad and fruit. But all the while, I am disappearing. I fade and fade, and then I am entirely gone.

— ◆ —

One of the house church couples, Grant and Mindy, belong to a national Christian leadership program. They have a spiritual book club and a deep desire to recruit more future Christian leaders, and one day, Grant has a little chat with Andrew about the whole thing. We receive a letter a few days later, explaining all of the benefits, the joy of becoming the Future of the faith.

And if there had been no deviation in my life, no heartbreak, no halting questions creeping up in my mind, I could be Mindy right now. I could be reading three spiritual how-to books while raising God-fearing kids. I could be mentoring girls in the way of true spirituality, taking pages of notes at Bible study discussions. I have been that girl; there is always the chance that if something hadn't gone awry, I could still be her.

As it is, I am not—though I am trying very hard to pretend to be. I am sitting on the old, ripped-up couch in our apartment when Andrew hands me the form letter from Grant and Mindy. I look at him, panicked at the thought of what sounds like a boot camp for Christianity. "We don't have to do it, do we?"

He gets a little sad half smile on his face. It's not really that he wants to do it, but I can tell he is a little alarmed lately by the sharp decline in my interest, my growing disconnect with the house church. He loves it here, loves the informal movement as we work our way across the western suburbs of Minneapolis, one house to another. He loves his men's Bible study and the mishmash of potluck foods every Sunday night. It is what he has always wanted, what he always believed church could be. I can tell he feels powerless as I drift, as my voice fades out of Sunday night conversations.

"Nah," he says casually as I take the letter. "It was nice of them to think of us, though."

I look at the letter. Words jump off the page. "The Lord has put you on our hearts...think that He could use you mightily...believe that this might be His will for you... Please prayerfully consider..." I look at them until they blur, and the lines cease to form words, but rather small wobbly patterns, void of form, void of meaning.

Andrew and I have been attending the house church for less than three months when Bill and Sheila decide it's time to split in two. It's getting too big for the kind of group they want, and the whole purpose of this kind of small house church is to reproduce. To split and split and split until there are hundreds of little house churches in the city of Minneapolis...little underground communities.

It's a nice idea...but the cost is high: more severing of relationships. The decision to split is made abruptly, and when I work up the courage to tell Sheila I feel blindsided, she says matter-of-factly, "Well, this is what the Lord wanted us to do."

I don't say much more about it. I don't know how to frame the argument, and I've lost the desire to fight.

For Andrew, the move is awkward but manageable. For me, it is a kind of death. The house church splits, and it creates two craggy cliffs. I am on neither one of them. I am *there,* eating my pasta salad quietly at Tom and Janet's house. Andrew is holding my hand. His thumb is tracing my fingers, but I can't feel it. I read a verse aloud mechanically, but I can't hear my own voice. I am there. I am not there.

I am gone, disappeared, lost entirely to the in-between.

I am a gray particle, floating. I am drifting into the void.

Fifteen

Community: A group of other believers whom you know
well and see regularly, and with whom you work out your
faith in deep and honest ways.

"S uper-Christians have kidnapped my husband," I type in a new online
chat window.

On the right side, the window interface shows photos of the partici-
pants in this conversation. The photograph on top is from Kim's last vacation to Rome. She's sitting on the edge of a stone fountain, her red hair
long and curly against her shoulder, her hand raised like one of the marble
statues behind her. Alissa's photo is below, and her face is filling up the
frame completely. Her brown hair is pulled back to show off yellow
feathery earrings. Her eyebrows are raised and her dimple is showing, and
she looks as if she's up to no good.

"Shit," Alissa writes, without missing a beat.

"Double shit," says Kim.

It is the beginning of November, and snow has just started falling in
Minnesota, where I am feeling far from my best friends, isolated in my
own little pocket of corporate America. Alissa is in her office in downtown Chicago, where she does PR for a radio station, and Kim is somewhere in the Chicago suburbs, editing medical books. We all have careers
that are a far cry from the ones we actually *want*. But we all have comput-
ers. We all have Windows Live Messenger chat.

The Super-Christians I'm talking about are the people from the
house church, and the truth is, they're not really Super-Christians at all.

They're just people, some decidedly strange, all imperfect. But I have been feeling so displaced in their group, a little unwanted, entirely unneeded. Meanwhile, Andrew is thriving. He is with the house church guys all the time, it seems, meeting them for men's Bible study and for spur-of-the-moment games of Risk.

So I write, "Super-Christians have kidnapped my husband" because I am feeling passive-aggressive. It's the first thing I do after I flip on my computer…before I've even checked my work e-mails or looked at my Outlook calendar to see if I have any meetings. I've come straight from Caribou Coffee, where I spent the last hour writing about it in my prayer journal, trying to get some perspective, trying to hear the voice of God in all of this. Instead, the mix of caffeine and exhaustion and hurt have spun themselves into an indignant anger before I've even eaten my granola bar. Before I've even checked People.com to see what the beautiful people are up to.

I look back at my screen. Kim has written, "What happened?"

"I don't know," I write. And it's true. I don't really know why this is bothering me so much. "They just *love* him there. It's like he's their king or something." I grab a granola bar out of my snack drawer and slam it for good measure.

The guy on the other side of my cube wall peeks over. "Everything okay over here?"

"Fine," I say, not making eye contact.

The chat window light is blinking. Alissa has written, "Where? At house church?" They both know about our search for the right church family. They know it's been hard on me. They understand this in a way other people don't, because in the last couple of years, they have both drawn away from their faith. It happened for each of them in a series of small, barbed interactions with Church People and a number of large, painful interactions with life. They know I'm still hanging on, white-knuckled, to my big church hopes, so they don't tell me the reasons they finally let go of theirs. Instead, they let me journey.

"Yes," I write, "at house church." I wait a minute, then write, "It just sucks. He's got all these friends there, and I can hardly get the girls to talk to me."

"Bitches," Kim says.

"You need us," Alissa writes, and I *do* need them. I need them to be in my house church. I need to be able to find refuge in their friendship. I need to talk about my faith with the people who have been there from the beginning.

"I know," I write finally. "I hate that we live so far away."

I sigh. Nobody types anything for a couple of minutes, and the weighted silence makes me a little weepy.

I wipe the wet corners of my eyes with my palms. "Anyway, I'm so ready to come home," I write.

"Are you coming for Thanksgiving?" Alissa asks.

"No." I sigh. "It's Zierman year for Thanksgiving. But I'm home for Christmas."

"Well, that's not too long," Kim writes.

"I know," I write, but it feels long. It feels terribly far away. I glance at the calendar hanging on the wall of my cubicle. It is a black-and-white collection of the photography of Robert Doisneau. The theme of the calendar is *Happiness*. In the picture for November, a pack of young boys in Speedos hang in a giant clump on a rope. They are swinging together with wide-open smiles. They will let go of the rope and plunge together into a great, rolling river. When they come up, they will be laughing, splashing, alive. "Just a month," I write. "Just one more month."

Part Three

Rebellion

Sixteen

Lost: A word describing a nonbeliever—a person who has yet to find Christ. This terminology emphasizes the before-and-after view of faith. Lost, then found. Blind, then seeing. Dead, then alive.

January

For a year of Thursdays, I meet the Church Ladies for morning Bible study at Coffee on Broadway. It is a bungalow-turned-coffee-shop on Main Street in Robbinsdale, and the door sticks a little when you open it against the cold Minnesota air at seven in the morning. The man who runs it has a full beard and a solid, daily routine. He watches the morning news on a tiny television set while pouring milk from a carton into my coffee.

This morning, Lindsay Lohan has made the news for checking herself into the Wonderland Center for rehab. I am standing at the counter, unzipping my puffy ski coat, stomping my black boots, removing my hat. The man with the beard is clanking around behind the counter. I am the first one here, and the only other sound in the place is the smooth voice of a coiffed blond reporter on the tiny television set. She is standing in front of the rehab center talking about Lindsay Lohan's alleged alcohol problems. A picture of Lindsay flashes on the screen. She is blowing a kiss to the camera, to her skeptical public, to everyone in the whole world, to no one. Her eyes are heavily mascaraed and half closed and strung out–looking. When I look at her, I want to wrap my arms around my own small, cold body. I think, *God, she looks tired.*

I am twenty-three. I have been in a downward spiral for two years now…ever since China. I don't know yet that I am sliding toward Depression. I think the darkness in my head is directly related to the darkness of the winter and that, come spring, everything will thaw, and I will be myself again.

Behind me, someone jerks at the sticky front door and fumbles in from the cold—Lisa, one of the young moms from the house church. "Hey," I say, turning from the story flickering against the screen.

"Hi there!" She is in sweatpants and her blond hair hangs straight at her shoulders. "How was your week?"

"Oh, fine—," I begin, but Lisa is distracted by the coiffed reporter and by the photograph of Lindsay Lohan. She watches for a moment and then turns away.

"Ugh," she says, under her breath. She looks at me and turns her voice to a conspiratorial whisper, "I wish he would turn off the news." She nods toward the bearded man who is bent down, fishing for something behind the counter.

I glance briefly back at the TV, at the girl with the frozen kiss and the heavy, sad eyes. "Yeah," I say to Lisa, while the bearded man clears his throat and sloshes the mug of coffee toward me. "It's really depressing."

February

I am falling. I am dead weight, and there is no one to catch me.

I don't think *Depression*. The word seems categorically reserved for the truly broken, and I have no good reason to be depressed. There has been no blunt trauma to my life, nothing I can point to and say, "Here—this is why I'm so sad." People go through great tragedies every day and bear nobly up under enormous amounts of pain.

I have nothing like this, but somehow Depression has found a way into my life through a different door: *loneliness*. Without a circle of protective love around us, we are no match for the shadows that stalk toward us in the night.

I start with the wine.

I learn quickly that Starling Castle Riesling is my favorite. I know my husband, a master of moderation, will say something if I drink too much, so I learn to slide into the kitchen when he is preoccupied and refill my glass in secret. I learn to love the feel of the cool wineglass against my hand, its skinny stem resting against my fingers. I learn to taste the different layers, crisp and complex and sharp against my mouth.

Most of all, I learn to love the feeling of being pulled up out of my slow dive, even if just for a night. I am drinking, and it is a parachute that seizes my falling body…and lifts. I am weightless. I am floating, and the world is small and fuzzy and a million miles beneath me.

March

The Church Ladies want to read the book of John, so Sheila picks out a Bible study book. Each question in the book has a narrow space for a prescribed answer. My answers are complicated, filled with questions, filled with doubt and frustration. They run out of the spaces and into the margins.

"Who wants to tell us what they wrote for question four?" Shelia asks one Thursday morning. We are sitting at Coffee on Broadway, and the room is filled with the sickly smell of potpourri. I look at my book. Question four asks, "How would you explain the meaning and results of receiving Jesus?" In the narrow space under the question, I have a large question mark.

Lisa has an answer. "It means your sins are forgiven, and you're not separated from God. You're redeemed. Jesus has made His home in your heart, and you don't have to ever be lonely anymore."

There are nods all around. I look down for a minute, trying to decide whether to enter the conversation. "I don't know… the part about Jesus and not being lonely?" I say finally. I look around. Lisa takes a sip of her tea. "Just—are we sure that's true? Because I…it doesn't always feel true."

"Well, we can't really go by feelings," Sheila says. "But that's interesting, Addie. Thanks. Let's move on to question five."

She doesn't mean to be callous, doesn't even realize she is coming off that way. Very few of us are good at entering into another's pain, at putting down the book midquestion and wading into the dark truth. Question five is about the order in which Jesus chose His disciples. It has a clear answer, so much easier to address than questions that are unanswerable.

— —

I start asking the Church Ladies out for coffee one at a time. I think that maybe if I can get them alone, I can find a way in. Maybe if one of these women is sitting across from *just me* at one of those small little coffeehouse tables, she will see that I am not doing well. I need someone to look at me and ask, with concern in her voice, "Hey, are you doing okay?" so that I can let myself break.

I meet with Sheila first. I ask her about her new house and about her job. I mention that I'm having a hard time with the Bible study on the book of John, and she looks a little offended. "It's what everyone wants to do," she falters. "I'll tell you what: you can help me pick out the next Bible study book we do, okay?"

I try to meet with a couple of the young moms, but they come late and leave early, leaving me alone with my thoughts and my paper coffee cup. They need to get home to husbands and kids and busy morning routines.

I meet with Janet last. She is older and has been divorced. She has been roughed up around the edges. She has been through her share of pain, and I have things I want to ask her. Such as how she kept it together when the world came crashing down around her. If she thought her divorce was a result of getting married too young, because I am just starting to realize how young I was when I got married…how young I still am.

But I can't get a word in edgewise. She wants to talk about her daughter. Her daughter's great success in college, and her daughter's future prospects, and her daughter, her daughter, her daughter. Then she wants to talk about her own job, her new position, and the difficulty of managing her peers.

I should break in midsentence. I should say, "Janet...I am falling. I am dead weight, and there is no one to catch me." But I don't know how to say it. I don't have the language to articulate the growing darkness I feel. I don't know why I am sad, only that I can't seem to shake myself out of it. So I sit, nodding, listening, sipping my coffee wordlessly until all of a sudden she realizes the time and abruptly leaves. I stay in the chair, holding my coffee cup, staring at the gas fireplace, watching the flames flicker aimlessly, powerless to ignite the fake logs below them.

April

One April evening, the split house church reunites for a special worship night. The two halves come back together after a month apart, but somehow, they no longer fit quite the way they used to.

The guitar guys play song after song, and the small circle of voices feels close and familiar and beautiful. I could almost uncurl into it. Stretch out a little. Rest.

The kids are there with us that night, and among them are two four-year-old boys who are jumping circles around the room. For them, this a safe place. These are their people. They run toward a couch, sit down, and then, propelled by the weightlessness of their senseless glee, run off again. Back and forth it goes, and I am surprised to find myself smiling.

But then Bill looks pointedly at Janet. She looks pointedly back. And then they step into the center of it all and pull those kids to the side. Janet bends down, says something in one of the boys' ears, and then holds sternly to his shoulders. I watch his face. I watch it redden and then distort. And there's something about the whole exchange that feels intensely personal, and it almost bowls me over, the weight of it.

The beat of the song picks up, but the four-year-old boys don't move. They were joy personified. They have been wrestled into stillness.

— —

That night, Andrew and I drive home in the dark. On 494, the cars glide steadily by, and I can't stop shaking. I rant. I swear. I redescribe the scene to Andrew to make sure I saw it right. He shakes his head. "It wasn't good," he says, and the frustration at the edge of his voice mirrors my own. "Who cares if the kids are running around? It's *worship time.* That's exactly what they should be doing."

"Right!" I say, and I feel vindicated by his words, his agreement. For the first time in months, we're looking at the house church and seeing the same thing.

"It wasn't good," he says again. "Just—no."

I roll down the window, and the late winter comes rushing in at sixty-five miles per hour, and you can almost smell spring at the edge of the cold wind. It feels like a turning, and I grab his hand and hold tight. He squeezes back. It feels as if everything is about to change.

— —

Every Thursday at morning Bible study, I have been pouring less milk from the bearded man's cardboard carton into my coffee mug.

By April, I am drinking it straight black. Black and rich and bitter. Black like truth. Black like reality.

By April, I am ready to leave the Church People.

— —

When I tell Andrew that I need to leave, I think maybe he'll understand. But he doesn't. Our shared disappointments with the church have been frustrating to him, but still, just a setback. A difference of opinion. For me, it was a shattering.

After work, he regularly winds his way through rush-hour traffic and ends up at one of their houses. They sit around the living room, Bibles propped on their open laps, dissecting, debating, asking questions of one another and of themselves. Then, afterward, they haul out the game of Risk and drink Mountain Dew and take over the world.

He doesn't want to leave. He doesn't want more unfamiliar church foyers and welcome packets and sermons. He wants this, these guys, this nomadic congregation of believers, the accompanying imperfections—he wants the whole thing.

He wants to know *why* I have to leave, and I can't give him a logical answer.

This is another thing about Depression: it seems to exist somewhere outside of language, and I cannot wrangle it. I can't seem to wrestle it into a manageable size using the thing I have always been able to use: words. I reach into the great cloud of unnamed feelings, but no matter how I try, I can't find the one true thing.

I try to draw it. We are sitting on our couch talking through it again. Should we leave? Should we stay? I pick up a sales letter from a Realtor that came in today's pile of junk mail and turn it over on our garage sale coffee table. "It's like this: the house church is on this path." I draw a straight line across the white paper. "And I am here." I draw a line curving downward, away from the straight-and-narrow of the house church. In the black ink of my Pilot pen, the departure of the Addie line seems abrupt and unforgiving, even to me.

Andrew is quiet for a minute, looking at the picture. He chooses his words carefully. "Why do you think?" he says.

I shrug. "I don't know," I say. I look at him next to me; I feel the strain of this on us, on our marriage, on our friendship. I don't know why I have slipped so far from the place where he is, but I don't think it's possible to hoist myself back up. "I'm just afraid that if we keep going to the house church, you'll be here"—I point to the house church line with the cap of my pen—"and I'll be down here…and I'll be all alone."

Andrew looks at the paper for a long time. I can tell from his face that he still doesn't understand. But he loves me. He loves me. *And.* He loves this church. I can see him battling as he thinks about it.

Finally he shrugs his shoulders. "All right," he says. "If you need to leave, I guess we leave."

———

When I tell Sheila that I'm leaving, she looks at me, surprised. "Why?" she asks.

"I'm just lonely," I say finally.

"Well," says Shelia, looking concerned, "if we had *known* you were lonely, we would have done something. We all thought you were too busy for us."

I'm sure, in this moment, that she's telling the truth—that she honestly didn't know. That none of them did. But I can't forgive them for not seeing it. For not seeing *me*.

"I'm sorry," I say, even though I'm not quite sure why I'm apologizing. What I want to say is that for a *year of Thursdays* I have met with the church ladies at Coffee on Broadway for morning Bible study…and still not one of them ever even *asked*.

Instead, I cry, give her a hug, and walk out of the coffee shop into the biting April air.

May

We've left the house church. Sort of. *I've* left the house church. Andrew continues to attend the Tuesday night guys' Bible study and the Thursday night house church leadership group. He is working on a technicality. *Technically,* he's no longer attending house church. On Sunday nights, he punches the video game controller, and I can tell he wishes we were there, eating pasta salad and hotdish. *Technically* he is supporting me in my need to leave…but he is hardly here. We are breaking apart a little more every day.

I start frequenting Don Pablo's with my coworker Robin after work. She went to Northwestern College too and, like me, emerged with a certain degree of cynicism. The bartender looks like Uncle Fester, but he is kind, and he remembers that my happy hour favorite is a margarita on the rocks. It comes in a big, heavy glass with salt around the rim and a green straw and a lime. I drink it quickly so the tequila slams into my brain.

The first time we go, I drink three margaritas. During the first one, Robin and I talk about Northwestern…the Lifestyle Statement we'd had to sign, stating that we would not drink or dance during our enrollment there. We have this gnawing feeling that a vital piece of our coming-of-age was stolen by so many unnecessary rules.

After the second margarita, the part of my brain that filters my thoughts has toppled, and I am telling Robin everything. I am talking about the Church Ladies and about Lindsay Lohan and about loneliness, deep and penetrating and unaffected by the presence of a husband or the stability of marriage. I am swearing. I hardly ever swear, but I can't seem to help it. I am wondering what the *fuck* is going on here.

After the third, I am crying into the basket of chips, deep, gut-level sobs. Uncle Fester is looking concerned at the bar. Robin is holding my hand and tossing angry, drunken slurs toward the Church People who are not there to see this pain or be appalled by this behavior.

June

I start to think that maybe it was just *that* church, those *particular* people. One night when Andrew comes in from an evening with the house church guys, I look at him angrily and say, "We need to go to the *same* church." I crank open the screen of my laptop computer and type "Churches near Plymouth, MN" into Google. "It's like I quit the house church, but you're still there." Andrew looks at me silently as I wait for the search engine to spit out a list of results. "Here," I say, picking the first church on the list. "We're going here."

Andrew says nothing, but on Sunday morning he gets up and drives us to Faith Evangelical Free Church. It is big and white and filled with the new faces of more Church People, who stand around the foyer, drinking coffee from Styrofoam cups and hovering above reality.

I think, *I am lonely.* The Church People say, "Let God be your Friend." The piano swells. A guy with long hair strums the guitar while the congregation sings "What a Friend We Have in Jesus." Jesus seems unresponsive. God is a million miles away.

I think, *I am Depressed.* The Church People say, "Trust the Lord. He will see you through."

I think, *I need a friend.* The Church People tell me to get involved with the women's Bible study. I go twice, sit with a group of forty-year-old Church Ladies while a blond woman preaches from the outdated television screen. Afterward we are to go around in a circle and answer the question, "If you were a fruit, which would you be?"

I drive away at ninety miles an hour because the words are empty and they are closing in on me. I am screaming and screaming and I am drowning, and the Church People are talking about fruit.

━━

I learn the art of drinking and driving: the careful grip on the steering wheel, the forced focus of mind on the road that is *not* moving. *I am not drunk,* I tell myself. *I can do this.* I squint my eyes, keep my foot steady on the gas pedal. *I can do this.*

When I get home I try to pretend I am sober, but Andrew sees through me immediately. I've stopped sneaking the second and third glasses of wine, started drinking them outright. We have been fighting about my drinking for weeks in that half-assed way we fight. He says something; I say something...and then we sink into the heavy silence of arguments unspoken.

Exasperated, I ask, "Why are you mad at me? Because I had a drink?"

"That's part of it."

"Well, what's the other part, then?"

"Drinks two and three."

"It was over the course of three hours. I'm *fine.*"

"You're *not* fine, and you know it." He sighs, looks at me. I can tell he is disappointed. "Look, there's nothing wrong with drinking...it's not a big deal. But getting drunk is."

"What is so damn bad about it?" I ask violently, but I already know. I have seen the after-school specials. I've heard the stories. I've seen Lindsay Lohan staggering back into rehab this month for the third time. And I know the science of driving drunk, the way alcohol affects the brain and makes you incapable of quick, good decisions, incapable of moving along a straight line, one foot in front of the other...

And yet I also know that it makes you brave. It makes you say the things you can't say and do the things you can't do, and I don't have the words to explain to Andrew the way it feels to have courage coursing through my body...even if it's contrived. Even if it comes from a bottle of tequila.

"It just *is*," he says finally. "It's just a really big deal."

— • —

I learn to make myself throw up after drinking too much.

I wake up in the night feeling sick and stupid, trying to reconstruct the pieces of the evening before in my mind. In the bathroom mirror, my pores are big and gaping under the glaring light, and I am filled with disgust for the person looking back at me. I bow before the toilet, and it feels like a prayer, like a purging. I stick my fingers down my throat as far as they go. I learn the feel of my gag reflex—that secret button that releases everything that I've ingested. I learn that vodka burns more coming up than going down.

Andrew is in the bedroom, sleeping. I hold my own hair back, and then, when it's over, I press my face against the cold white porcelain until my head stops pounding. I lean back against the bathtub and make promises to myself. *I will never be like this again. I will never be like this again.*

I wrap my arms around my legs. Everything is quiet. I listen for God but hear only the dishwasher whirring on the rinse cycle. *Shhh. Shhh.*

July

We spend the week of our birthdays driving up the East Coast, from New York to Maine and then back down again in a rented car. We've been planning this trip for months, and we don't talk about house church or about the strain of it all. Instead, we read the final book in the Harry Potter series to each other over the sound of the wind whipping around the car. We walk around the Yale campus and along the crowded cobblestone of Providence, Rhode Island. We drive the scenic routes, stopping to take pictures of small stone walls and old, sprawling houses. We eat ice cream. We walk hand in hand into the icy waves of the Atlantic as sea gulls soar and circle overhead.

We drive fast enough to keep the sadness mostly at bay, but every now and then it catches up. Like on the night before my birthday. We spend the whole gray day walking through Salem, Massachusetts, which has a sort of ashy sadness about it, and that night I drink the entire bottle of wine. I get silly, and then I throw up in the space between the hotel bed and the wall. I wake to my twenty-fourth year deep in a foggy hangover.

At a small local bookstore in New Hampshire, I pick up a book by Sue Monk Kidd called *The Mermaid Chair.* I am thinking it will be like her first book, *The Secret Life of Bees,* filled with deep, spiritual symbols and hope and redemption. Halfway through, I realize it is not—it's about a marriage dissolving. I can't bring myself to finish it. Instead, I focus on the sea that laps alongside our car until we get to Maine and then head back by way of Vermont's Green Mountains. The road winds, and the sun streaks into the car, and I put down Harry Potter and say to Andrew, "I think that when we get home, I need to find a therapist." My voice breaks a little when I say it, and I am surprised to realize I've been holding back tears all this time.

Andrew doesn't turn to me when I say this, but focuses on the road ahead of him. "Yeah. You should." In the way he says it, I can hear his unfailing support, his deep love for me. In the way he says it, I can hear his confusion, his hurt, his desperation to find the woman he married.

August

Andrew is with the House Church People again. I am at Caribou Coffee. I am sitting in the black faux-leather chair. The man sitting next to me is not my husband.

I'd rolled back into town resolute about getting well, about finding someone to help me. I'd browsed through the in-network therapists at work, but it felt thick and unfamiliar. So many names. So many practices. I closed the window and drove home without making an appointment. Instead of getting help, I started getting coffee.

The man at the coffee shop is, of course, not really a man at all, but a boy. His name is Brad, and he's twenty-six, unemployed and unmotivated and coming off of a bad breakup. One day, I ask him to help me with an Internet problem, and that's all it takes. One smile, one conversation. We are, both of us, broken; neither of us is willing to admit it.

Brad spends his evenings at Caribou watching YouTube clips, every hour exiting through the jingling front door to lean against the window and smoke. He spends his nights drunk on Jägermeister, and in the morning, when I am knee-deep in software documentation at work, he is sleeping off the hangover in his mother's basement in the suburbs.

He never finished college, and he drives a junky red car with a back-seat full of garbage. It sports a "Fueled by Caribou Coffee" sticker along its bumper; rust streaks like birthmarks across the trunk.

He is shorter than I am by maybe a couple of inches. When we stand, our height difference coupled with the way he angles his body close to mine make me a little uncomfortable, but most of the time, we are sitting. We are sitting next to each other almost every night in those black leatherlike chairs by the gas fireplace at Caribou. He is telling me that I am beautiful, and suddenly I'm telling him the whole jagged story. He is staring into my eyes, listening to my heartache, telling me that the House Church People are crazy not to love me. "I mean, who wouldn't love you?" he says, and I ignore the brokenness in his voice when he says it. He touches my hand, and the whole thing sends a wild jolt to my brain.

If I were healthier, I would not have needed this. I would not have even noticed him, sitting across the room the first night that I came into Caribou, looking for an escape from our empty apartment, from the buzzing silence of my husband's absence, from the knowledge that he was with the Church People on a straight line far from my pain.

He knows I am vulnerable, this man who is not my husband. He senses it the way a shark senses blood in the water, and he edges closer to me. I am not healthy. I like the company, the attention, the devotion. I like the way he looks at me when he speaks the half truths I am desperate to hear. It makes me forget he is short and he lives with his mom and he is always a little bit hung over. It makes me forget I am sad. It makes me forget I am married.

———

The man who is not my husband comes with a built-in set of friends: evening regulars who are young and single and who sprawl easily around me on the Caribou furniture. Without a word, they absorb me into their easy, benevolent friendship. It's as if I am one of them, have always been one of them, and I like the way I don't have to prove anything to them.

Too quickly, I make them my family. My house church, circled around the chairs in Caribou, talking about nothing, conversation volleying easily back and forth. I trust them immediately, mostly because they are not Church People, do not use the language of evangelicalism, do not say the words that have hurt me.

— ▬

One night, I get to stay at Caribou until closing. Andrew is across town, at a hotel where we have just attended the rehearsal dinner for one of his cousins. He will spend the night there with his family, his cousins—all guys his age, all his closest friends.

I do not belong to them, but I belong to Caribou, so that's where I go.

We sit and talk until we close down the place, and then we move the party outside. The night air is warm, the parking lot almost empty. I am still wearing the black polka-dot dress, and the tug of the warm wind against the fabric makes me feel free and lovely. I can feel the gaze of the man who is not my husband on my legs, and it all still feels mildly innocent to me as I flip my long hair over my shoulder and gaze toward the cars gliding west.

When the coffee runs out, we walk, all of us, across the parking lot to a restaurant, where I order two-for-one margaritas. The shift in location is jarring to me. I have known these people only in the context of the Caribou, where their friendship is available and yet contained—restricted to this one small space. I have known Brad only inside the Caribou, where his flattery and come-ons feel illicit but mostly harmless. Where I know that at any time, I can walk out the door and leave him behind.

But now, it is as if Pandora's box has opened, and this world that was so well kept has flown out into the darkness. Brad sits next to me, his shoulder unnecessarily against mine, and I drink my two margaritas so fast that the restaurant begins to sparkle with so many stars, so fast that I begin to slide in the booth.

When we leave the restaurant, I am wobbly in my heels. The moon is half there, and a storm is beginning to rumble across the sky. Every now and then, there is a wide flash of lightning, illuminating everything. One by one, my Caribou friends disappear into the night, making their way home. They take with them their laughter, their light conversations, until it is just Brad, telling me how beautiful my eyes are. I am drunk on margaritas and on the moment. I am watching Brad touch my arm, watching him lean in close, inhaling the nicotine on his breath, realizing that he is about to kiss me, about to really *kiss* me…

I realize that this is going to happen if I don't stop it, and the realization jerks me back to a harsh reality. I back away.

Brad apologizes. He is pitiful, lovesick even though it's not love. I *know* it is not love, just some drug, synthetic and addictive. I give him a brief hug, kiss him fast on the cheek, and send him away. At home, I sleep fitfully, waking crying and nauseated throughout the night.

In the morning, I break periodically into uncontrollable sobs as I clean my house and get ready to go to the wedding across town. I am crying because I know I should not go back to Caribou, but I will anyway. I will go back because I need them, because too quickly I made them my family, my house church, because I have learned to rely on them for friendship and community and strength. I have grown used to the way the lies of a man who is not my husband wrap around my pain. I am not sure I can survive without these things.

— ◂ ▸ —

I tell Andrew about the almost-kiss at the wedding as we sit at a small, round table in the reception hall. The place is clearing out, but the bride and groom and most of the kids are still dancing. He nods but doesn't say much. If he feels angry, he doesn't show it. He mostly looks at me silently, and nods, nods, nods.

He is taking in my red-rimmed eyes, unable to understand the complexity of feelings causing this endless stream of tears.

In the almost-empty reception hall, Andrew and I dance to the last song. We hold on tight to each other, and we don't say anything, and I want it to be enough.

I put my head on his shoulder. His hair is businessman-short now, but I can remember it big and curly underneath my fingers. The early days ring through my memory like some distant bell. I look at him, and he looks at me, and we are so far away from each other. We are two separate lines, and no matter how hard we try, we can't seem to intersect.

We dance close, and I remember the bundled-up Northwestern walks. The glove-in-glove in the snow. Pink noses and disapproving RAs and sweet good-night kisses in the stairwells.

I remember *happy*. But I am on a line descending into some deep-down darkness. He is somewhere else, somewhere I cannot reach. I am losing him, losing us, losing myself. I am falling, and I can't find the way back.

— • —

Over the next days and weeks, I continue going to Caribou, just as I knew I would. I tell Andrew that Brad is not there, when really, he is. He always is. Brad is staring at me sadly, making up reasons to touch my hand. Then, one morning, Andrew picks up my journal. He takes it into the bathroom and reads about That Night, about the kiss on the cheek that I gave to Brad as we parted ways.

It is this act, this kiss on the cheek, that jolts him into understanding and makes him furious. Suddenly, it all becomes clear to him—the way in which I have grown to depend on this one relationship, on this man who is not him—and in one blinding moment, he understands.

He comes out of the bathroom, his eyes red, and holds up the journal.

I scream at him for reading my personal diary, and he waits, looking at me sadly. When I finally stop shouting, he looks at me and asks, "Are you still seeing him?"

I wait a moment, and then answer, "Yes."

This is what "rock bottom" looks like: your husband who never cries is crying. He is gone, walking the paths around your apartment, trying to manage the pain. You are alone with your heavy, broken heart and you don't know how to fix any of it.

—▸—

What happens next is the slow climb out. I stop going to Caribou entirely. Andrew spends extended time with his friends talking through it all.

What happens next is my first foray into individual therapy. It's the telling and retelling of the whole complex thing until I find someone who looks at me gently and says, *Okay. Let's begin here.*

It's a Depression Checklist in a quiet waiting room and a visit to the doctor for antidepressants. He prints out the prescription and then draws a diagram of my brain on the back. On the diagram, the synapses are misfiring, the wiring in my mind shorted out for no explicable reason. I start with one pill a day. They are white and feel chalky going down.

Andrew leaves the house church—*really leaves*—and he makes the appointment for marriage counseling. That first Tuesday night, we drive in silence to a towering office in St. Louis Park. We sit at opposite ends of a small couch and stare at a wall of old family Christmas cards. We explain the whole situation to the petite blond woman from the photos. She looks at us kindly while we sit side by side, separated by a space that we can't navigate.

She waits until we finish and then says gently, "I think you're going to be all right. You've hit a rough patch, and we have to find a way to get you through it. But I honestly think you're going to be all right."

September

I call Kim and Alissa and tell them I need an emergency girls' weekend road trip. To Memphis. It feels just random enough and far enough and exotic enough to work. They cancel their weekend plans and order an official TripTik trip planner from AAA. We are all feeling a little exiled. It hasn't been that long since Kim's visa expired and she was deported from London, the city she loves. The city where her serious boyfriend lives. Alissa is getting over her first love, a tall bear of a guy who unceremoniously dumped her a few weeks back over the phone. We could all use a girls' weekend away.

We are feeling the toll of life as we drive to Memphis in my white Hyundai Accent over Labor Day weekend. We eat Triscuits with spray-cheese along the way, and I cry and tell them everything. When we get there, we do our hair and head to Beale Street. Arm in arm, we drink slippery nipple shots. We drink rum and Coke. Vodka and cranberry juice. Vodka and Red Bull.

I drink right along with them, even though I know you're not supposed to mix the antidepressants and booze. I do it on accident and on purpose. I do it because I got used to the art of self-sabotage, and because sometimes it's all too much. Because I'm with my best friends. Because it's Beale Street.

We drink and drink until Alissa is passed out in the back of the cab and Kim is spouting nonsense on the phone to her long-distance boy-friend, and I am tearily babbling to the heavyset driver about the problems with Christians while he says, "Mmmm hmmm, mmmm hmmm, mmmm hmmm."

On the last night, we go to Bar Louie, where, of course, it was a mistake for me to drink four and a half glasses of wine. I should have stopped when I first noticed the colors blurring, the streetlights streaking bright against the August night. But we were sitting at a high table on a patio filled with young, happy people. It made me thirsty.

And something profound happens four and a half glasses of wine later, when you have come crashing into a wall you forgot existed inside of you. When everything is fuzzy and you can feel yourself being stupid, talking loud, making a fool of yourself. When you go staggering into the public rest rooms, crumple onto the dirty floor of a stall, and throw up.

Grace.

This is it: your two best friends leave the table, cram themselves into the grimy bathroom stall, and hold you, your shoulders, your hair, while you are sick. Sick not because of some outside force—the flu or motion sickness. Sick because of the force of your own pain and stupidity and the combination of both on a sticky summer night. You are puking, and it is disgusting, and they are sitting with you, brushing your hair away from your face, saying, "It's okay...it's okay...it's okay..."

— —

It is hard after I get home from Memphis. Loneliness is aggravated by the brief window of friendship. I cry every day in my cubicle.

One Friday I come home, red-eyed and tired, and Andrew pulls me into his arms and says, "Let's drink margaritas all night."

"Really?" I look at him suspiciously.

"Really."

"I'm a pretty sad drunk."

He laughs, "It's okay."

We drink the margaritas fast; the alcohol hits me in waves. I am giggly and tipsy, and then we are naked, and then, I am crying. We are skin on skin, wrapped around each other, and I am crying because the alcohol has stripped away everything that was holding me together.

"I'm sorry," I whisper. "I'm sorry."

"Shhh." Andrew is laying me down on the floor. He is kissing my tears and my cheeks and my lips, wrapping his fingers in my hair, covering me with his warmth. I am shaking from sadness, and he is there, holding me steady.

"What if I never get better?" I ask.

"I love you," he whispers.

"What if I'm sad forever?"

"I love you. I love you. I love you."

"I'm not worth it. I can never make you happy."

"I Love You."

He whispers it over and over, whispers it into my skin until the words make me shiver and my broken soul opens to receive love. Grace. Life.

October

We are Working on Our Marriage. We enroll in a ballroom dancing class on the top floor of the Plymouth community center, and some weeks we skip it for no good reason. We sit, instead, in the garden below in our jackets and hats and watch the couples move, shadows and silhouettes against the wide windows.

But mostly we go. We learn to dance. Every week, we pay less attention to the steps, not because we've figured them out, but because they matter less and less. The teacher gives up correcting our footing and just lets us go.

We move erratically around the room. There is no really good reason to laugh, but we can't seem to stop laughing.

One weekend, we drive to Taylors Falls, a tourist town on the St. Croix River. A little getaway. An oasis.

We stumble upon an old house from the 1800s for sale, and spend twenty minutes wandering around peeking in all the windows. On a whim, we call the Realtor on the sign. He comes and unlocks the door, and we move slowly through old rooms. We look at musty bathrooms and battered drywall and our Realtor points out a hot tub balanced illegally on the roof. We laugh and decide it is too much for us, this broken, beautiful house on the river.

But we also decide that we should look—really *look*—for a house, and it feels sudden and unexpected and entirely perfect.

We'd been trying all this time to find a "church home," and we'd failed in the most heartbreaking way. It seemed right in those crisp moments of early fall to begin looking for a different kind of home—one we could build and inhabit together.

So we walk hundreds of empty rooms on the weekends. We notice tile and woodwork and built-ins and paneling. We talk about what we'd change. What we'd keep. What we love and what we hate. We work our way in from Taylors Falls, getting closer and closer to the Cities every weekend. We don't care much where we live or how long it takes to get there. We are noncommittal. Picky. Not sure of what we want, only what we don't want. What we *need*.

But I begin to see it a little bit more clearly each time we open a new door: a different life. A new future. The sunlight glints off of empty countertops and old wooden floors, and it's muted but *there*—a cautious bit of hope.

— • —

I begin to frequent the Har Mar Pet Shop during my work lunch hour. I have never had a dog, and I cannot ever remember wanting one, but I need something to hold on to. Something small and furry with a rough pink tongue that licks my face again and again. Something with a tiny heartbeat racing toward me with all sorts of pent-up love.

The windows in the pet shop are small and have tags stuck beneath them indicating each dog's price and breed and birthday. The puppies are tiny and unnamed and alone in their windows, but they are jubilant with hope. A shaggy black-and-white dog sees me and begins to claw at the window. When I hold him, I feel as if something inside of me is being restored. I go home that night and tell Andrew about the puppy while he looks at me, mouth open. He keeps saying, "Really? You want a dog?" He tries to gauge whether I'm serious.

We go back the next day. Buy the dog. Name him Marty.

Each day after work, I drive home fast. I am thinking of the puppy, caged in the kitchen, waiting with his tail wagging for me to come home. I forget to look at the Caribou Coffee looming on the east side of the road as I pass by, forget to miss the people there. When I get home, Marty jumps and jumps and pees on the floor a little bit. I put his leash on, and we take long walks on the trails behind our apartment, and for the first time, I begin to notice the colors: the leaves turning orange and red and beautiful around me. The tenor of the sky changing in the cool autumn air. Marty runs back and forth, exploring it all, and just being attached to him—to his energy, to his small strength—is enough for now.

At night, the dog curls up against the inside of my bent knees and rests his soft head against my calf. I feel surrounded by warmth. Andrew is breathing next to me, and Marty's breath is coming in small puffs against the back of my sweatpants, and I too am breathing in and out. I am aware of it for a while, and then I become less aware of it...and then I am asleep.

November

It is winter again. I am slowly pulling up, out of the darkness. The doctor is pleased with my progress but has opted to increase my dosage to two pills. Every night, I brush my teeth and swallow them down hard.

I will be drunk again in the future, sometimes on accident, sometimes on purpose. But the last time I try to drink away the sadness is November 30. I do it with four vodka-crans and one cosmo at a downtown bar. I do it because that day at work, no one spoke a word to me, and somewhere along the line I learned to drink the loneliness straight down.

I drink because "getting better" is a labyrinth, and part of the whole messy thing is this circling around your struggles. At some point, I always come back around to my lonely heart. The circles get wider with time, but always, there is this unexpected returning.

So that night, I drink myself numb and embarrass myself at a poetry reading. I swerve drunkenly home down 694; I stumble, drunk and sobbing, into the Caribou, where I am not supposed to be.

The man who is not my husband, whom I haven't seen in months, stands up and stares at me. But the barista on duty that night is Miles, a quiet kid from Northwestern College, my evangelical alma mater. Without waiting for me to order, he fills a white mug with my favorite coffee—on the house. Without waiting for me to ask, he guides me by the elbow to the black leather chair in the corner. My old spot. Without saying a word about my tears or my slurred speech or the fact that I have clearly been driving across the city drunk, he takes my hand in his. There's no trace of hidden desire in his touch, just gentleness.

"Why do Christians suck so much?" I ask loudly when I can finally speak, because the moment of striking loneliness always brings me back here. To church. To the places where I am most wounded. I look at Miles, angry, my breath a mix of alcohol and dark roast.

"I don't know," Miles sighs. "They just sometimes do."

I put my coffee down and put my head in my hands.

"I know what you're going through," he says quietly. "I mean, I've been there."

"Why did you go back?" I mumble into my hands. I mean to the faith. To Church People. To the college on Snelling with the required biblical studies major and the ridiculous visiting hours and the rule about not dancing. To the people who look at you suspiciously, who wait for you to fail.

Miles thinks about it for a moment. "Because some of them don't suck. Some of them understand what Jesus is all about. Some of them will love you without a thought."

A fresh wave of tears starts for no reason I can understand, and Miles waits, this college sophomore in his black barista apron. He should be up front working the register; he'll probably get in trouble for this later, but still, he stays with me. His presence keeps at bay the man who is not my husband, who is lingering at the edges of my brokenness, waiting. Miles waits until I have composed myself enough to drink my coffee.

"You're going to be okay," he says softly.

"How do you know?" I ask. My hand shakes as I take another sip.

"I just do," he says and shrugs. Then he stands and holds out a hand. "Come on," he says with a soft smile. "Let's get you home."

— ⬩ —

I get home late. It's a weeknight, and Andrew has to work the next day. But he is lying in bed with all the lights on, forcing himself to stay awake. When I walk in, he gets up and wraps tired arms around me, and the dog jumps around us, and I am safe, and I am held, and it is grace.

I'm sure he can smell the alcohol and the coffee mixing on my breath, but he doesn't say anything. Instead, he looks me in the eyes. "Come to bed with me, Sweetie," he says. "Come to bed."

December

In the new Caribou, everything is all wrong. Windows stretch wide over the walls, and the cold December air beats against them and pushes drafty cold into the coffee shop. In the new Caribou, the gas fireplace sits broken in the middle of the room. The comfy chairs, the faux-leather ones, are pulled back from it, uncomfortably close to one another. I can't sit with my feet propped onto the stone base the way I used to at the old Caribou. I can't feel the warmth creep across the bottoms of my jeans like before.

I am not really that happy to be here. But I have to be somewhere. So I sigh, walk up to the baristas who do not know my name, and order a coffee.

"What size did you want?" the shifty seventeen-year-old girl asks me. She looks bored with her job and with me, with my boring black-coffee drink order. Her hair hangs in a messy ponytail, her black Caribou apron tied loose in the back.

"Just…a mug," I say.

"Huh?" she asks.

"One of the mugs, please." I point behind her to the row of white ceramic mugs sitting on top of the coffee maker.

Bored High School Girl rings up my order with an agonized sigh. When she sets the mug down on the counter, coffee sloshes over the edge.

The only chair open is one of the black faux-leather ones. It is positioned next to the other black one, in which there is a man—a young man, probably my age, who is holding a computer on his lap. I approach the chair sideways, careful not to look at him as I sit down, as I place my coffee cup on the table, as I riffle through my bag and take my own laptop out. Open on the desktop is iTunes, revealing my Melancholy Playlist. Songs with sad titles: "Waiting for My Real Life to Begin." "Fix You." "World Spins Madly On."

These are the songs that have formed the soundtrack of my life lately, pumping into our apartment through the computer speakers or into my head through my headphones, always coursing through me like a mantra. I was listening to it before I came here, while I did the dishes and wrapped presents and packed myself for Christmas up north with Andrew's family.

He left yesterday to get in a few extra days with his cousins, taking me in his arms before he left. "You sure you'll be okay?" he'd said into my hair, and I'd nodded. "Fine. I'll be fine."

I have been sponging up the silence he left in his wake, holed up in the apartment with the dog while snow falls outside.

Christmas Eve is a mere three days away, but it doesn't seem to matter. I want to listen to Pete Yorn instead of "Jingle Bells." Patty Griffin and Colin Hay instead of "Joy to the World." I can't handle the way the Christmas songs repeat on every radio station and pour down on me from store speakers, their characteristic bells jingling obnoxiously overhead. I am still a little bit broken; I am still not ready for this.

All around, people are wishing one another a white Christmas. "May your days be merry and bright…" I can't remember what brightness looks like. Everything in my head still feels so dark. So today, I drove to a tanning salon, the gift certificate in my purse an early Christmas present from Andrew, who knows I am desperate for light. I went to lie in the tomblike silence of the tanning bed, stickers over my eyelids and muffled Christmas music pouring in over the walls. I went to be warmed by fluorescent light, to let it pour its deep, destructive rays into my body until my skin burned red.

Now I'm at Caribou, and I reek of coconut. My skin has an unnatural glow to it…probably because the radiation is still coursing through my veins, ravaging my insides. I'm in sweats and a ponytail because it didn't seem important to shower today.

Now I'm sitting next to some guy. Now he is talking to himself.

"Hmm…," he says loudly. "I just don't know."

Great, I think, *he wants to chat.* I glance sideways at him, trying to make an educated guess about him based on his attire. Most important, I need to know if he is just a guy, just striking up harmless conversation with a girl in a coffee shop, or if he's one of the Skeezy Guys. If he can sense my vulnerability and see the ways in which I am still not quite healed. If, even upon seeing the wedding ring glittering on my finger, he'll try to start something.

I would guess him to be in his early thirties. He has a goatee and jeans and a beanie-style cap with the name of a Christian band on it. *Switchfoot.* I know it well from my high school days. It graced my CD rack along with other Christian "rock." I try to remember if I've been to a Switchfoot concert, but the past feels blurry and piecemeal in my head.

I can't decide if meeting a goateed Christian with a Switchfoot hat is better or worse than meeting one of the Skeezy Guys. So I turn back to my computer and try to look busy.

But Switchfoot guy does not get the message. He turns to me, says, "Hey, do you know what *yuletide* means?"

"I don't know," I say, looking at him reluctantly. "Isn't it the same as Christmas?"

"That's what I'm trying to figure out," he says. He looks at the last line of the e-mail he's been writing. I peek over his shoulder at the Yahoo! mailbox open on his screen. "Could I say in this e-mail, for example, 'May your yuletide be full of merriment'?" He reads it carefully and politely and then looks to me for affirmation. His seriousness is disarming.

"Sounds fine to me," I say.

"I'm going to Google it." He pauses, clicks a few times on his computer. "Aha. Okay. 'Yuletide: the twelve-day pagan celebration worshiping the sun.'" He turns to me. "Probably not a good way to end an e-mail to Church People," he says.

I smile. I like that he said *Church People*. "Probably not," I say. "Church People don't like pagans. And they're real suspicious of the sun."

He is drinking from his paper coffee cup when I say this, and he laughs midswallow so that his face turns a little bit red and he has to work hard to get the coffee down his throat. I can't decide if I'm more pleased with my cynical wit or by the fact that Switchfoot Guy is not currently giving me The Look—the one that includes equal portions of concern, judgment, and disgust. The simultaneous scrunching of the eyebrows and widening of the eyes. I've gotten The Look a time or two before.

"So," he says, wiping coffee flecks from the edge of his mouth with a napkin. "You've had some run-ins with the pagan-hating, churchgoing type?"

I shrug. "I've been burned by my share of Christians."

"That sucks," he says.

"Yeah, it's kind of shitty," I say. I add the *shitty* on purpose as a kind of a test. I've been using it a lot lately to weed the dangerous Christians out of my life: the ones who have the power to hurt me. Throw out a *shit* or a *damn* or a *what the hell,* and see if you get The Look. Watch to see if the person shifts uncomfortably or looks down at her hands...then you know: this is a Dangerous Christian. The kind who will not be able to handle the truth of your pain, the kind that requires some swearing. So I say, "Yeah, it's kind of shitty," and then I watch Switchfoot Guy. He looks at me, interested, waiting for me to go on.

When I don't, he says, "Yeah, churches can kind of blow. I actually used to be a, uh, youth pastor."

"Used to?" I shift in my seat just enough so that I can look at him properly.

"Yeah…shitty church politics," he says. He uses the *shitty* like a sort of verbal wink. I can see what he's trying to do. He's trying to say to me, *We're on the same side.* It's like I'm a deer standing stone-still in some forest, and he is coming toward me slowly. He's trying to say to me, *It's okay. Don't run. I'm not going to hurt you.*

"I couldn't deal with it anymore," he continues. "So much drama, you know?"

"So what do you do now?"

He grins. "Actually, I make documentaries."

"Really?" I say. "What about?"

"Poverty. And what our response should be as Christians."

"Cool."

"I guess it's kind of about motive," he says. "It's about how we should respond to crises in the world, like poverty, from a place of *love.* Not, you know, like a duty or obligation or whatever… Because if you do that, it comes off as pity." He spins off into a tangent, but all I can think of is that I am sitting across from the first Christian that I've met in a year who realizes that pity and love are not the same thing.

Outside, the wind beats its white breast against the earth, slamming itself against the windows around me so that they rattle quietly in the background. It is Christmas, but also it is yuletide, and it seems to me that maybe this is sort of fitting. Both, after all, are a celebration of Light come down.

I can feel my face reddening still from the tanning, and it seems as though maybe this is an okay way to celebrate Christmas. That maybe this is the way you move on. You find the small slivers of light, and you hunker down in them. You hole up in the still warmth of this kind of beauty and you wait, knowing that the beams will get wider and wider every day. Knowing that one day, you will wake into the full power of the sun, and you will finally be warm.

Seventeen

Faith Journey: A metaphor for the Christian life; it is meant to communicate that people move toward God at their own paces and accounts for differences in opinions, understandings, or choices.

S ee, this is the problem with politics," Kim said, carefully refilling her giant margarita glass, then looking to see if Alissa and I needed our glasses topped off. We did.

"What is?" Alissa asked, swallowing a bite of her pizza and holding her glass steady for Kim to fill it.

"You need the Republicans because they like to go to war and take out the bad guys. But then, after that's done, you need the Democrats to come in because they're the ones that get people educated and like... fed...and stuff."

It was, of course, a gross oversimplification of the inner workings of a complex political machine, but we were two margaritas in. It sounded like the most brilliant thing ever said, and Alissa and I looked at Kim wide-eyed and nodded. We were all dolled up. Our earrings jangled as they moved.

It was January 2008. We'd just seen *Charlie Wilson's War* at the Desert Star cinema in the Wisconsin Dells. We'd draped our feet over the empty seats in front of us and eaten gas station candy that I'd stashed in my purse, and we watched Tom Hanks somehow convince warring political parties to do the right thing for the world. Outside, the winter air was brisk, and presidential candidates were starting to campaign, hoping to represent their parties in that year's presidential election. We were caught up in all of the political fervor. We were talking about it over a pitcher of margaritas at the Pizza Pub. We'd recently realized that we knew so little about politics or economics or foreign affairs. More important, we realized we *wanted* to know.

Most of the people we knew had gotten their drunken political conversations over with in college. Most people had settled into a political identity by twenty-five, but in college we were learning the cultural history of Leviticus and trying to navigate a shifting spiritual spectrum. We weren't quite ready.

So we were doing the typical college experience a little late. In spurts. A weekend here, a weekend there, most of them taking place there, in the Wisconsin Dells, the halfway point between Chicago and Minnesota.

We always stayed at the Days Inn with the free tanning beds and the big hot tub. We borrowed each other's clothes and earrings and then drove laughing down Main Street, past the roller coasters and the water slides, past the giant pink flamingo and the big, lopsided haunted mansion. Past the petting zoo and the Indian trading post until we got to the Pizza Pub, where we'd become acquainted with the local bartender. Where he made us a pitcher of extra-strong margaritas so that we could dissect everything from faith to politics. We let it all unravel on the tall bar table. We poked at it between hot bites of pan pizza. We weren't so bitter anymore, not the way we were in Memphis, but we were curious. We had a lot of questions.

"I feel like such a grownup, talking about politics over margaritas," Alissa slurred. Her dark hair was cut short and she'd curled it expertly at the ends. Between the curls and the dark red lipstick, she looked a little like a 1940s pinup girl.

"I feel like I never used to think about any of this stuff," I said.

"Yeah." Kim tossed her long red curls behind her shoulders. "Everything was a given. We were kidnapped by the Super-Christians."

"Damn evangelicals," Alissa said with a mouthful of ice.

"In my bag right now, I have three magazines," Kim said, and it felt random but somehow related. "*The New Yorker, Elle,* and *The New York Times.* I feel like this means I am a grownup."

"Wow," I said, a little jealous. "When do you have time to read three magazines?"

"Airports. Flights to London." Kim was still living unhappily in America, making frequent trips back to England to see her boyfriend. She was working three jobs, trying to make the powers-that-be renew her visa. She was always a little tired, always a little sad.

But not that night. We were, after all, in that small, strange oasis in Wisconsin. We were back together, finishing each other's sentences, drinking margaritas, and it was a kind of healing, a kind of momentum. We were doing the things we needed to do to move forward.

"I want to get *The New York Times,*" I whined. "And *The New Yorker.* And *Elle.* Why don't I get any magazines?"

"You should get some." Alissa pointed her fork at me for emphasis. "I think you need magazines."

In those days, I was in the business of rebuilding my broken life. I was still seeing the therapist. I was spending a lot of time with the dog, going on long walks through the snowy winter nights, music pulsing in my ears, Marty tugging at the leash.

Andrew and I had recently made an offer on a cute split-level in the suburbs. On my way out of Minneapolis that weekend, we'd learned that our offer had been accepted. By the end of the month, the place would officially be ours.

It was another step toward *getting better.* I was starting to feel the color returning to my face. And tonight, over margaritas, my faraway best friends were there, helping me navigate the new normal. They were encouraging me to wear earrings, to buy magazines, to take care of myself.

"I should," I said. "I will."

"Good," Kim said. "Now flag down the bartender. We need more margaritas."

Eighteen

Prayer Life: The part of one's daily life devoted to focused conversation with God.

I don't want to pray," you tell your young, brown-haired therapist in one of your sessions. You are defiant about the whole concept, the word itself trapping you in a sticky web of bitterness.

Once upon a time, your prayer life was a vibrant collection of journals, each filled with small, cursive letters—your prayers. Here, in these journals, your every emotion was laid bare, tempered with humility and the desire to be more like Christ. They fill a giant Rubbermaid container, which you stash in the storage room at the new house along with the Christmas lights. Sometimes you take them out to remember what it felt like to say, "I'm overwhelmed, Lord. Help me to rest in You."

You fold your arms. On the wall of your therapist's office is a framed degree from a local Christian college, and you glare at it, even though you picked her on purpose. You wanted to talk to someone who understood, firsthand, the intricacies of an evangelical past and who could help you sort through the whole mess of it. You're not sure you want to discard your whole complicated faith, but you definitely want to untangle yourself from some of its stringy implications.

"I just don't think I can," you say. "Pray, I mean." Your eyes flicker over her and then back to the colorful squares on the carpet.

"That's okay," she says. "You don't have to pray. You may find that you can relate to God in other ways."

— ▪ —

The April of your sophomore year in high school, two boys brought guns into a high school in Colorado and took the lives of twelve of their peers and one of their teachers. Then they turned the guns on themselves and ended their troubled lives. You remember the chaos this day created in you as the news spread to your corner of the Midwest. You remember the way your heart lurched when piecemeal stories began to circulate about the girl who was shot that day when she told the killers that, yes, she believed in God.

You organized a prayer rally. You stayed up all night pinning white ribbons to small square fliers that you distributed the next day at school. When you stood that night around a flagpole with a great crowd of your peers, holding lit candles and praying aloud, you felt as if the world could absolutely change in this moment. That this rally with its growing numbers could be the catalyst for some kind of revival.

In those days, prayer was largely associated in your mind with Action. Movement. You imagined God's hand, giant, draped over the landscape of your world. You imagined your prayers, rising like steam, disappearing under the callused fingers, under tough, wrinkled skin and slowly lifting it.

You wonder now where you got this idea, because it doesn't seem to be from the Bible. The Bible says on prayer, "When you pray, do not be like the hypocrites, for they love to pray...on the street corners to be seen by men." The Bible says on prayer, "Go into your room, close the door and pray to your Father, who is unseen." But the evangelicals passed out "See You at the Pole" T-shirts and said words like *revival,* and you learned that this is how you pray: loud, desperate, in the company of many.

You understand that your journey now will include unlearning this. It will be about creating a new picture of prayer to hold in your hands.

— ▪ —

When people confide their deep hurt to you these days, you are at a loss for what to say. A long time ago, you used to say, "I'll be praying for you," and you always meant to do that, to take those heavy burdens off their shoulders and hoist them up to the Lord. But the truth is, you usually forgot. Usually, this was the thing you said to end the conversation, a nice way to say, "I'm sorry. I can no longer handle the depth of your pain. I don't want to talk about this anymore."

These days, you don't say much of anything. It feels dishonest to promise prayer when your own life still feels so heavy on your shoulders. How could you bear their sorrow in addition to your own?

"I want you to know I'm praying for you," your mom says on the phone one day, and a knot of emotion gets stuck in your throat. You know she means it in a way you never did, never could, because her prayers are motivated by love, while yours were prompted by obligation.

But she is your mother, and you are her heart, and if she could be there with you right now, she would. She would give anything in her whole world to make things better for you, to make you happy again, to restore light to your dark heart. But she can't and she knows she can't, but she believes with all her heart that God can. She will sit up at night in her armchair. She will keep watch over you with her prayer. Her words will reach across the distance that separates you and hover over you like angels as you sleep.

— ◆ —

You learn somehow about 24-7 Prayer, an international prayer vigil that spans continents and cultures, a vigil that meets in a great diversity of places: "the US Naval Academy, a German punk festival, war-zones and underground churches, the slums of Delhi, the jungles of Papua New Guinea, ancient English cathedrals and even a brewery in Missouri."

You never attend a gathering, but you explore the website for a long time, and you're intrigued by a quote you find: "We encourage people to [use] creative mediums to help people find new languages to engage God in conversation. Some speak, others think or sing, many write, lots find expression through paint or sculpture."

"I don't want to pray," you'd said.

"That's okay. You may find that you can relate to God in other ways."

Somewhere in Berlin or in Tokyo or in Missouri, someone is painting a picture in a prayer room. Someone is writing in a lined journal, and there is no template, no secret, no need to speak warring words aloud.

Someone is sitting in the quiet, pushing clay between her hands, and God is listening, understanding, reaching across the void. It is nothing like what you are used to. But still, it is prayer.

— • —

When you start to finally pray again, it looks like this:

It is winter, and you are walking your dog. The moon is bright. Full, maybe. There is a certain quality about the light that is streaming down onto the white snow. The trees are glazed heavily; the snow is powdery, and the dog is flinging himself back and forth across the pathway. He is running as far as his leash will allow, then stopping to roll in the cool of the snow.

Under the hood of your coat, you are wearing headphones. "Transatlanticism" by Death Cab for Cutie is playing. It is a slow song with lots of piano and space for thought. You feel the sound wash over you, cleansing.

The dog bounds toward you and licks the snow off your gloved hand. He cocks his head, waits for you to rub his ears, and then takes off again. The song moves into the bridge. A simple refrain, over and over: "I need you so much closer."

The dog pulls on the leash, and you walk forward. You whisper the words along with the music: "I need you so much closer." You feel the words in your soul like a kind of desperation and feel yourself reaching for God. He feels big tonight. You can sense Him in the whitening sky, a kind of quiet nearness, a familiar voice. Safety. He is coming near; He is saying, *I'm here. I've always been right here.*

The music is filling your ears, pumping down into your body, and you are reaching forward, filled with the thinnest trace of hope.

—● ▬

It is difficult to tether your mind, your soul—a struggle to find a way into the great mystery of prayer. But it occurs to you that you are part of a great, vast company of seekers, and you realize that there are so many traditions, so many different avenues into this kind of life-giving dialogue. There are other words to use to talk about prayer, words you never learned in your evangelical upbringing: *meditation, contemplation, mantra, lectio divina, prayer of quiet.* These words fill your heart with warmth.

You finger prayer beads in a shop one afternoon. When the Church People you have known have mentioned beads or rosaries, they have done so with pity for those who need them, those who don't understand that you can talk to Jesus as a friend, those who repeat prayers over and over, void of meaning.

But that day, you have the urge to buy those beads. To find a way to connect your body and your soul as you embark on the slow journey back toward God who is Love. You are beginning to understand the circular nature of prayer, spiraling toward a tiny center and then curling out again.

To learn to pray is to learn to walk this labyrinth again and again, in and out, in and out. It is to be filled with honesty and determination and love, to learn to walk circularly through your whole life toward the Light at the center that never stops burning.

Part four

Redemption

Nineteen

Baptism: The immersion of oneself in a body of water as a way of symbolizing the transition of death to life in Christ.

Oh my God. This is amazing," Alissa moaned. She eased her body into the hot, bubbling water, the steam rising into the muggy night air above. "Why don't I have a hot tub in my living room?"

"Because you live in a loft in Chicago," Kim said.

"Right."

"It sucks that you can't get in, Addie," Alissa sighed. She closed her eyes and leaned her head back against the side of the small pool, letting the water cover her shoulders and bubble at her chin.

"It's all right." I shrugged. I was sitting at the edge of the hot tub, my long shorts rolled up, my bare feet skimming along the top of the water.

"You don't want to boil Baby Z," Kim said.

We'd been in Florida for three days, which meant it was three days before that I'd found out. It was three in the morning, and I was getting ready to leave for the airport. I thought, *Maybe I should just double-check,* and pulled out a pregnancy test. I'd taken one two days earlier, and it had been negative…but I was Late, and it was Girls' Weekend in Florida, which meant sun and alcohol and sun and alcohol, repeat, repeat, repeat. It meant three days of irresponsibility. It would be good to know if there was a tiny start of Someone for whom I might be responsible.

I texted Kim and Alissa from a shuttle bus as I rode from the overnight parking lot to the terminal in the pitch-black morning. *On my way to the airport,* I wrote. *Also, pretty sure that I'm pregnant.*

I took a second test in the bathroom of an Italian restaurant in downtown Clearwater, just to be sure. I was fresh off the plane, and the test I brought out to the restaurant patio had two lines also, nothing blurry or uncertain about it. "Oh. My. God," Kim said.

"No way," Alissa said.

We all giggled, breathless, amazed. The waiter came out a few minutes later to tell us about the specials, to tell us about the town of Clearwater, that Tom Cruise had a home just up the beach, that it is the Scientology capital of the United States, that we should be careful not to go swimming after sunset because of the sharks. I listened and nodded but was silently aware that the world had shifted suddenly, indescribably, unmistakably beneath me.

———

Alissa's feet broke out of the bubbles. "This was just what I needed after today."

"I still can't believe we went to Disney World," Kim said, laughing.

"I know. Best seventy-five dollars I've spent in a long time." We had decided to go on a whim when the morning turned out to be too gray and drizzly for the beach. We were driving aimlessly around Clearwater, and then we were suddenly on the highway, headed toward Orlando, headed toward the Happiest Place on Earth.

We'd arrived just in time for the morning parade down Main Street, U.S.A., elaborately decorated floats bearing our favorite Disney characters. There was music pumping through the streets and children waving, and we were standing there together, the three of us, crying sentimental tears as we watched it all unfold in front of us.

We spent the day riding the magic carpets and the teacups; we'd stood in line to have our pictures taken with Mickey and Minnie. We'd tried on hats in every gift shop; we'd crammed together in a small cart to tour the Haunted Mansion and then again to see the dolls wave and remind us over and over what a small, small world it is.

At the end of the day, I'd picked out a onesie from a Disney gift shop. "All aboard for fun!" it said. I would give it to Andrew when I got home. I could already see it unfolding: him holding the onesie, trying to make sense of it, staring at it a long moment before that *click* of understanding. The crushing hug. The surprised *What!* The big, dimpled grin. I could already see it all.

"Honestly," Kim said, scooping a handful of foam off the surface of the water and holding it in her hands. "We should make this an annual thing."

"We totally should," Alissa agreed, and I nodded, though we all knew that it would never happen. Kim's visa had been approved, and in a few months, she'd be moving back to London. Permanently. Soon the Wisconsin Dells would cease to be the island refuge between our homes; instead, it would just be some strange town with too much kitsch, just some place we used to go. Soon I would have a little baby, and I wouldn't be able to leave spontaneously for weekends at a time to get wasted on margaritas and laughter. Soon, everything would change.

We were quiet, thinking all the unspeakable truths. Kim said suddenly, "I can't believe we never went skinny-dipping in the ocean."

Alissa dipped her head into the hot water and then came up. "We couldn't," she said, wiping the water out of her face, slicking her hair back. "The *sharks,* remember?"

"Still," Kim said, "it's our thing."

"I know."

"It is our thing," I repeated, looking at my friends.

"Fuck it," Kim said. She jumped out of the hot tub and began ripping off her swimsuit. First the top went, then the bottom, then she was running across the concrete toward the outdoor pool; she was flying into it with a great splash. Alissa and I were shrieking, our voices bouncing loud off the hotel walls.

"Come on!"

Alissa scurried up the side of the hot tub and wiggled out of her teal bikini.

"You guys!" I whispered loudly. "Someone is going to see us!" All around the perimeter of the pool, sliding doors led to dark, curtained hotel rooms. Any moment a light could flip on, and someone could walk out, and we would be caught.

"Don't be lame, Preggo," Kim said as Alissa cannonballed, naked, into the deep end of the pool.

"Fine!" I pulled my feet out of the hot tub and started peeling off my shorts and my underwear. I was working my shirt off when the lobby door opened suddenly, and the guy from the front desk walked purposefully out onto the patio. He made it a couple of feet before he stopped short and stood frozen in place looking at us.

We all screamed. I grabbed my pile of clothes and ran for our door, trying to cover my ass with my hand. Kim and Alissa were hoisting themselves out of the pool. *"Shit!"* Alissa sputtered. *"Shit, shit, shit!"*

The night manager disappeared, clearly more embarrassed than we were, but we kept screaming anyway as we ran naked to our room, as we slammed shut the patio door, as we locked ourselves in and deadbolted the door for good measure.

Twenty

Shine: A hit song by the Christian pop-rock band the Newsboys, released in 1994. This song became something of an anthem for evangelical youth, and lyrics like "Shine/ make 'em wonder what you got" linked joy and happiness with an irresistible Christian witness.

So, I'm doing EMDR again in therapy," I tell my friend Robin. We've slipped away from work early today for happy hour and are sitting across from each other in our usual upstairs booth at Don Pablo's.

"EMDR." She thinks for a moment. "Is that the thing with the flashing lights?"

I nod, though it's not so much lights flashing as light gliding back and forth across a long, dark plank. It stands for Eye Movement Desensitization and Reprocessing, a treatment method used to process difficult memories. The idea, my therapist has told me, is to reprocess these memories using both the right *and* the left brain—adding logic and perspective until you understand that the event is in the past, know who or what was responsible for it, and no longer filter everyday choices unknowingly through the pain.

I don't really understand the mechanics of it. The bits of paperwork I read describe it as "the rapid 'metabolizing' of upsetting experiences." There are several other pages describing the process and the goals of various phases, but they are sitting, unread, on my nightstand. The idea of trying to make sense of it all feels exhausting to me. Somehow the idea that light leads to healing just seems to fit, so I choose to trust it.

"So," Robin says, "what are you EMDR-ing?"

"Oh. Chris—my evangelical ass of a high school boyfriend."

Her blue eyes widen a bit. "The guy who made you do all the push-ups?"

"The one and only."

"Oh, he *is* an ass."

Robin doesn't know tons about Chris, but the few tidbits she does know have been carefully handpicked to demonstrate his assiness. Like the time he instructed me to punish myself with ten push-ups every time I said something sarcastic. "Jesus was never sarcastic," he had said. "And you want to be like Jesus, right?"

"Well, good," Robin says, taking a sip of her margarita. "Any particular reason you're doing this now?"

I sigh. It has been several years since I sat by the fireplace at Kim's house, feeding Chris's pictures and mementos one by one into the flames...but still I can see his face as clearly as my own.

"I think I'm ready to stop hating the evangelicals."

"Now what's so bad about hating them?" She laughs.

It's a valid question. Our friendship has been formed primarily in the act of telling and retelling the ludicrous words and actions of various Church People in our lives over giant margaritas and bottomless baskets of tortilla chips. We have spent much of this year explosive with anger, our stories flying like fireworks—all noise and color. Acceptance was not on our radar, the act of purging too deeply satisfying to let go.

Except now, I'm pregnant. I'm sipping lemonade instead of a margarita. Part of it, I'm sure, is the change in beverages. Without tequila to fuel my righteous indignation, it sputters and dies much more quickly.

It's been more than four months now. The first three and a half were spent mostly bent over various toilets, enduring bouts of what I soon began to understand was not, for me, morning sickness, but *all-day* sickness. But now I have a bump. I have heard a heart beating fast like wings. This week for the first time, I felt tiny movements fluttering within me, rising like joy. And one day in May, that little baby boy will be born—an inextinguishable light, a little piece of immortality.

And my great fear is that, if I don't do something now, this baby will be born under the great, long shadow of my bitterness. I'm afraid that my lost faith in the goodness of people will create a cold, gaping emptiness where there should be only love.

Outside the window, the streetlights come on. The day is darkening, even though it's only four thirty, and flurries of snow are moving frantically along the shadows. Winter is here, with Christmas following swiftly behind it.

"Don't you find it...exhausting? Being so angry all the time?" I ask finally.

"I guess." She shrugs.

Our regular waiter, Mike, comes to the table to see if we need refills. Robin orders another drink, then she and Mike get into a lively discussion about the merits and shortcomings of particular brands of beer.

I look out the window at the long string of streetlights gliding down the street in front of us...as if staring at the glow will loosen the grip of those memories, that they will somehow come untangled and fall away from me like the snow.

— • —

I sort of missed Christmas last year.

I know we had a tree, but I don't remember putting it up. I don't remember seeing the lights on homes or hearing the bells by the red kettles at grocery stores.

It had been only a few months since the thing with the house church. First there was rage. After that, sadness, heavy and unyielding.

At the Christmas Eve candlelight service when the congregation sang "Silent Night" a cappella in the darkness, I didn't sing along or pay attention at all, really, as the candles moved smoothly back and forth across the church pews. People looked each other in the eye and repeated

in hushed reverent tones, "Jesus is the light of the world," and I was somewhere else entirely.

— ◆ —

"Okay," my therapist, Rachel Martin, says calmly once my coat is off and
I'm comfortably folded onto her white leather couch. "Let's check in.
How was this week?"

This is the first thing my therapist says to me when I come to her
office. Not "Hello." Not "How are you?" No small talk. No shenanigans.
Just right down to it.

After more than a year of therapy, her directness still feels uncomfortable. When I talk about her with my friends, I call her by her full
name. *Rachel Martin*. Just "Rachel" seems too familiar, "Dr. Martin" too
removed. She is an entity all her own. Not a friend, offering witty banter
at the beginning of a session, but not a stranger either. She occupies an
ethereal place above the fray of my life, and our relationship is to the
point, focused on the healing work that still stretches ahead of us.

We have moved past the immediacy, the crisis point. I have been off
the antidepressants now for a few months, and I can feel myself getting
stronger. Healthier.

Andrew and I have lived four full seasons in the new house. We spent
months pulling down ugly wallpaper borders, scraping leftover bits of
paper off the walls, piece by piece. We repainted, redecorated, revamped.
One weekend, we spread out in the living room in our sweatpants, surrounded by vacuum-sealed Ikea furniture pieces. We were walking
through it step by step. Assembling.

We don't talk much, these days, about our last life. But some days I
feel it, a dull ache somewhere below the surface. It's worst when we attend the new church across town. We started going a few months back,
because it felt as if it was time, as if it was somehow essential to all this
recovery.

But when we go, I feel myself snap shut like a steel trap. Andrew drapes his hand across my back as we sit in the back row, and we raise our eyebrows pointedly at each other when anything feels off. Something trite is passed off as gospel, and I squeeze his hand desperately. The pastor cries for the third time this morning, and we roll our eyes in tandem.

In the foyer, on the way out, I find myself arms crossed, head-down, afraid. I am half daring them to love me; half afraid that they will.

So I keep plugging away with Rachel Martin. Every week we trace the thread of my faith slowly, carefully, until we find the next tangled place.

These days, we're working on the tangle that is Chris Jacobson.

Rachel Martin gets up and pulls the bulky EMDR machine from the corner of her office. It is a long, black instrument with dozens of little green lights spaced evenly from one end to the other. The lights come on quickly, one at a time, and the idea is to follow the movement with your eyes while recalling a painful memory and focusing on it. Rachel Martin lets the lights go for about a minute at a time. Then she stops the machine and says, "What are you noticing?" I tell her, and she doesn't comment except to say, "Let's go with that."

I've done this once before, the EMDR. Last time, we reprocessed a mild but somewhat defining kindergarten incident. It took one session of watching the lights to bring the power of that memory from a seven on the Disturbing Scale to a one, so I am thinking Chris should be nothing more than a harmless phantom by the end of today's session.

"Are you ready?" she asks.

She asks me to choose one particularly difficult memory of Chris, one representative of our relationship. This will be the fixed point of our session, the memory we will come back to—the piece of the knot we will begin tugging at in order to untangle the past.

"Yes," I say, gathering the memory into my mind. "I'm ready."

"Okay, then. Let's begin."

———

Lights start.

I am trying to watch the light and to focus on the memory at the same time. It takes time before my concentration becomes automatic and my mind is free to wander.

I see him. He is sitting on the end of his twin bed, cross-legged. He is looking at me intensely, with squinty eyes and pursed lips—his preaching face. I see him look down at the Bible on his lap. I hear him take a deep breath and say, "Look, it's about your clothes."

"My clothes?" I see my fourteen-year-old self like a separate person… young, innocent, hanging on his every word. She is wearing a striped Old Navy sweater over her thin, shapeless, freshman-in-high-school body.

Chris sighs. "You need to stop dressing so provocatively. I mean, I know you don't mean to, but it's still a sin…and it could cause your brothers to stumble."

I want to step into the scene now, to shake this boy-man as hard as possible. I want to make him see what he's doing, and then I want to put my arm around her, the girl who is me. I want to stop him from saying all of the things he will say to her on this night and on all of the nights after it.

But I am on the outside, past this time.

Both versions of me are crying.

"Here. This scripture explains it best," he says, opening his Bible to a bookmarked passage and reading: "'I want women to dress modestly, with decency and propriety, not with braided hair or gold or pearls or expensive clothes, but with good deeds, appropriate for women who profess to worship God.'"

The scripture appears in my memory word for word because that night, when I got home from Chris's, I wrote it in puffy paint at the top of my mirror. I wanted to make sure that every time I dressed I would think of Chris and of the Lord and I would make sure not to dress provocatively. "I'm sorry," I hear myself whisper.

"You just need to be more careful. A WOG is always modest," he says, smiling a little. WOG is his code word for "Woman of God," and when he refers to me in this way, I understand it to be the highest kind of praise. "A woman who flaunts her body is like the wayward woman in Proverbs...always setting traps."

Fourteen-year-old Addie nods, thinks *I'm a whore.* And then, *I will change. I can change. I will change, I will change, I will change.*

Lights stop.

— • —

Lights start.

I zero in on the image I have in my head of Chris. His piety is almost comical as he sits there with his Bible and his lesson on modesty.

It is easy now to see what the girl who was me could not: that this is not a good situation. That the words he is speaking are control words. That there is nothing wrong with my outfit at all. In the distance of time, Chris has become caricature, symbol. Gone are the complexities and the nuances. Gone is the feel of his hands, gentle as they held mine. Gone, the nights we sat across from each other at Steak 'n Shake. His shoe was soft against my shoe under the table, while above we ate french fries and said words like "grace" as if we understood them. It is easy to believe that the girl is stupid, that she should have *seen it,* that if she had been looking with her eyes wide open, she would have.

But manipulation is easy to conceal, easy to miss. It moves deceptively, camouflaged by a kind smile. A bouquet of flowers. A handmade kaleidoscope, *turning turning, turning.*

It can hide anywhere, even in faith. Even in religion. Even in the passing of scripture across a twin bed. The truth is that there can be a kind of veiled darkness masquerading as a conversation about light.

Lights stop.

— — —

Lights start.

I survey the boy and the girl on the bed—the boy with his preaching face, the girl, small and contrite before him.

I try to hold the image in my mind, but it cascades into a wave of memories tripping over each other in my brain, images flashing and then disappearing before I can grab hold of them and figure them out.

I am alone at the flagpole at Buffalo Grove High School, the rain dripping down my face, the boy I love far away in Texas, away at Teen Mania, learning to keep me at arm's length. I am cold. I hear Kim's voice: *"We couldn't figure out where you were!"*

Teen Mania. Rain. Falling. Wet. Cold.

Cold like the midnight air in Garden Valley, Texas. I am at the Teen Mania headquarters practicing the drama about that ship. I am wearing my black scrubs, my white mime makeup. I am standing on the lawn in the pitch black, shivering, while the director of Teen Mania shouts into a megaphone.

Someone screams and I feel it: downpour. I am standing, shocked, in the grass, looking out across the road to the intern dorms where Chris will live in the fall. At the intern dorms where it is definitely *not* raining. It takes me a minute to realize what this means. It means, of course, that this is not rain at all. That they've turned on the sprinkler system. That they're doing this on purpose, and that it's a kind of test.

The black sleeves of my formless shirt are clinging to my arms, wet, dripping. Clown makeup is running down my face, leaving thin white trails on my shirt. The Teen Mania director walks by with his megaphone, and I know he can see me shaking. I know that even in the dark, he can see I am crying. But he says nothing. He turns his body away. I am alone.

Alone.

I am alone in the church foyer, while Chris disappears into the familiar crowd—a folded-up letter in my hands. I am alone in my bedroom, the cordless phone next to me on my bed. I am sitting in the stairwell of my parents' house, my legs straight out before me. I am standing on a painted map of the United States on a playground at night, reaching my hands toward Texas. The boy standing there is not reaching back. I am writing in my prayer journal, "I know that he is just doing Your work, Lord. Forgive me for my selfishness. Give me the strength…"

I am standing in front of my high school again, and I see it clearly for the first time. There were two places to stand: an empty flagpole and a crowded hallway. I thought I was choosing something extraordinary; I did not realize I was choosing loneliness.

Lights stop.

——

Rachel Martin says, "Does your body need to react? What does your body want to do?"

"Beat the shit out of him," I say, half joking, half sobbing.

"Okay," she says, as if this is a viable option. She holds a couch pillow up, and I beat it as hard as I can while she says, "Yes. Very good. Yes," so calmly that you would have no idea that she was bearing the force of my anger. I punch the pillow over and over again until I collapse, sobbing, into myself, and Rachel Martin says, "Really good, Addie. *Really* good."

——

Lights start.

I think of the girl on the bed, who is thinking, *I am a whore.* I want to save her from who I have become. She has a soft, open heart. She's too naive, of course, but she loves freely. She loves completely, all the way down to the broken places in her heart. I try to remember what it felt like—the softness, the openness—but all I can feel is the wall I have built. It is pressing in on me, heavy on my organs. I look down and notice my arms crossed tightly in front of me. I try to let them flop to my side, but they are taut and defensive. They are poised to protect, but it's too late. That girl on the bed is gone. In her place, there is a cynic and a small, new life growing within her.

Lights stop.

——

Rachel Martin says, "You know, it's possible to have been in a cult without actually having *joined* a cult. Do you know what I'm saying?"

"Not really."

"Cults don't have to be groups necessarily. There is such a thing as a 'cultic relationship.' And it's not about beliefs or values; it's about the method they use to convince you to follow." Rachel Martin puts her clipboard down in her lap and looks at me gently. "Do you think Chris would have stayed with you for that long…for three years…if you hadn't so willingly obeyed him?" She pauses, giving me time to think it over, shake my head unsteadily.

"I'm sure he didn't realize it at the time, but it was like he was looking for someone vulnerable. And you were that person." Rachel Martin makes a few notes on her clipboard and looks at the clock. "We're going to need to end our time there."

"We're going to have to do this a bunch more times, aren't we?" I ask. "The EMDR?"

"Yes," she says. "This isn't like the kindergarten memory, Addie. This is big."

"I know."

"Change takes time," she says. I nod and hand her a check, and she smiles encouragingly. "I'll see you in two weeks."

— ◄—

When I get to the car, a few light snow flurries are dancing around the parking lot. The wreaths have been hung on the outside of the office complex where Rachel Martin works, and the guy on the radio is talking about a Christmas special that will be on television tonight. I snap off the radio impatiently and immediately regret it.

It is not silent in the office parking lot, and it is not night. I am late getting back from my extraordinarily long therapy lunch hour. But I lean my head back against my seat, sing "Silent night, holy night. All is calm, all is bright…" I sing softly at first, then louder and louder. I sing all the verses I can remember. I sing it over and over again…until somehow it starts to feel a little like Christmas.

— ◄—

By the time I get back to work from therapy, I'm hazy and exhausted. I should not be doing this heavy work during my lunch hours, but it seems to be the only time it fits, the only way I can work it into my life. I sit heavily in my chair and impatiently tap my mouse to wake my computer. No new e-mail messages, no meetings.

Clearly there is only one thing to do at a time like this:

Facebook stalk Chris.

I log into the social networking site, type his name into the search field…and then there he is…smashed into the small frame of a thumbnail photo with his blond, angular wife, Debbie. Although we are not official Facebook friends, I click on the blue hyperlink of his name. I fully expect to be redirected to an unfriendly error message, informing me that I am unauthorized to view his profile page. Instead, I am immediately admitted. I do a muted evil laugh under my breath. He has *open* security settings.

He has gained weight. This makes me feel immediately happier and somewhat vindicated. In his profile picture, he is not smiling, but rather looking intensely into the camera with squinty eyes and pursed lips and a patchy half beard. His preaching face. Under the picture it says, "I am in love with Debbie!" and tells me that he has 469 "friends." Both statements annoy me.

Some of the information fits. He is a member of groups like "God is moving in ISRAEL and I want to be part of it!" and "Lovers of Elisabeth Elliot Gren," a famous missionary wife whose husband was martyred by a hostile tribe in Ecuador.

But noticeably absent are the passionate overarching claims he used to make. I expected his "status" to say something like "Chris is living *every day* for the Lord—no regrets!" Instead, it says, "Chris is hangin' with Molly. Watching *Heroes*."

I scroll through black-and-white photos: Chris with his wife and friends in Chicago's Grant Park on the day Barack Obama was elected. When I knew him, he was staunchly conservative, but here he is, walking down the stairs to the el train. Here he's sitting in the grass with friends. Here his arms are raised in triumph as, in the distance, a very, very small Barack Obama steps up to give his acceptance speech.

There are pictures of Chris in Spain with a *bikini-clad* wife. Drinking *beer*. His arm draped around a guy who is *smoking*. On some of his postings and comments, I notice curse words, "damn" and "shit," and I immediately flash back to the look of disappointment on Chris's face when I used the word "crap" so many years ago.

And it occurs to me that maybe all of this time, Chris has been changing too. Perhaps the Chris I knew and revered—the boy who crushed me under the weight of his self-righteousness—no longer actually exists.

—◄—

I read somewhere that at week fifteen, your baby can sense light from the womb. If you hold a flashlight to your stomach, the baby will move.

I think about this as Andrew and I decorate our Christmas tree, a somewhat haggard spruce that we bought at the tree lot behind Festival Foods. There is no snow, but there is Christmas music playing, and we are both sort of half singing along.

I am holding a string of lit Christmas lights in my lap, trying to untangle them, and I think, *Maybe he can sense this.* I wonder if the string I am holding is glowing somehow through the skin on my stomach, and if this baby in my womb is aware of it. I want him to see it. I want him to know that he is surrounded by the movement of light. It is a process, but in some strange way, it is guiding us all.

"What are you doing?" Andrew asks, looking at me, staring at the lights in my lap and at my stomach.

"Oh, just hoping the baby will see the light and move around," I say.

"Any luck?"

"Not yet," I admit.

"Well, hand me those lights. I'm running out," he says. I lift the lights out of my lap, and we string them slowly around the tree.

Twenty-One

Born Again: A metaphor for spiritual rebirth that has morphed into a cliché, a cultural context, a way of stereotyping, an excuse for all evils.

The day he is born, there is light everywhere. It is streaming through the windows of your hospital room, and it almost takes you by surprise, the brightness of it. The whole thing began at one thirty in the morning, and the nurses kept the delivery room dark so you could sleep between contractions. The low lighting over the desk and the fluorescent glow of the computer screens barely slipped into your consciousness as you labored, your husband next to you, holding your hand, passing you ice pieces, touching your hair. *Breathe, breathe, breathe, breathe.*

And then he is there, and he is tucked into your hospital gown, and you are skin to skin, and you feel so luminous, as if you're lying in a sunbeam, as if there is a halo of light circling your beautiful new family as you lie in the hospital room, bloodied, battered, being stitched back together.

Born.

Somewhere in all of your prebaby reading, you learned that memory and oxygen are linked, that the former depends on the latter. That even in those first days of life, your baby can have no memory of his dark, uterine world, of kicking his tiny feet absently into your ribs, of his harrowing journey from that dark calm into the noise and light of your delivery room. To have memory, there must be breath. To have breath, you must be born.

"I tell you the truth," Jesus said to Nicodemus, the high-powered

Pharisee with a mild curiosity about the new Jewish rabbi. "No one can see the kingdom of God unless he is born again." Born of water. Born of Spirit. Alternatively translated, "born from above."

You imagine that this new metaphor was staggering in those first moments after it was spoken. The marriage of the most natural and messy of human processes with the spiritual. With God. This idea that everything before This Moment was dark and muffled, and now you have emerged into brightness. Clarity. Joy and understanding and light.

Here is how a metaphor becomes cliché: it is overused until it becomes the name of a national movement. The Born Again movement of the 1970s for example. A book is published by one of the great political schemers of your time: Chuck Colson of Watergate fame, who found Jesus during his time in prison and then wrote a best-selling autobiography about his experience. He called it, of course, *Born Again,* and the cliché was deepened. Cliché turned movement turned cultural construct. It began to characterize a certain kind of person with a certain political identity and a certain taste in music and a certain way of moving through the world.

I'm a Born Again Christian, said President Jimmy Carter in an interview with *Playboy. I've been Born Again,* said Johnny Cash and Dr. James Dobson and George W. Bush. George Wallace, best known for saying "segregation now, segregation tomorrow, segregation forever," became a born-again Christian in the 1980s. Apologized to black civil rights leaders for what he said Before. Before when he was in figurative darkness. Before he was Born. Again.

You can't decide why this particular phrase is so troubling to you. Something about the shift in grammar: verb to noun to proper noun, morphing into a caricature of itself. Something about the way it is wielded like a weapon. Defensive, to excuse all manner of evil: *That was before! I've been born again!* Offensive, as a way to write someone off, to group his beliefs into one small, laughable package, as in, *Those fucking born-agains…*

Yes, faith is like being born again. But it is also not like being born again. Unlike the newborn infant, the new Christian has memory, memory that spans back into the darkness from which he came. He is not so much born as waking…every moment to new realities. To a new way of looking at humanity. To grace and to peace and to love. It is not Before and After, a clean split, dark and light. It is gradual illumination, fireflies moving slowly toward you, softening the edge of the darkness so that you can see the beautiful mystery around you.

And it occurs to you as you look at your son's small, beautiful face that you never stopped believing any of it. Not really. Even in your raging, you couldn't forget that Story, couldn't deny the way it rang clear and true in your ears. It always made sense to you that there is a way to be in the world. That good begets good; that bad begets bad…that there's always that pull to run away. You fail, and you get drunk on the sadness and the hurt, and you fuck things up, and Love still comes. You can't always feel it, but it's there, always breaking into the darkness. And if you just keep moving toward it, that mysterious, beautiful Light, you'll find that slowly, slowly, slowly you're healing up whole.

You think about the void between the phrase *born* and *born again*, and it occurs to you that this story is too big for all of these words. The Christian-y ones that have been used so badly. The evangelical words-turned-weapons. They have grown so heavy; they groan, now, under the weight of all their baggage.

Take the word *missionary*. It is meant to describe a person who has given her life to serving others, who has uprooted herself and gone to the Need in order to help fill it. In the Merriam-Webster dictionary, "humanitarian work" is part of the fabric that makes up this word itself, but you don't hear that connotation anymore. You hear the director at Teen Mania, his voice booming in the loudspeaker. You feel red dirt cake underneath your fingernails and white paint on your face. It evokes a feeling of shame for you, the word *missionary*. It opens the door of a great emptiness, the realization that you have been left for something Greater. It smells like island rain and Aspen cologne. It feels slippery on your tongue like the white part of a hard-boiled egg. *Missionary.*

Take the word *saved* as it is used in the evangelical vernacular. It's true, you are saved by grace, by love, by light…but it's only half the story. The truth is that there is so much that you're *not* saved from. You are not saved from pain or loneliness or the bite of reality sharp against your skin. You're not saved from rained-out picnics, from disappointment, from the unkindness of strangers. You're not saved from lost jobs or lost loves or cancer or car accidents. *Saved.*

But they say, *It's not religion, it's a relationship.*

They say, *God loves the sinner but hates the sin.*

They say, *Let go and let God.*

And they're worse than cliché, really. They're *thought-terminating cliché,* a term that psychologist, Robert Lifton, coined in his book *Thought Reform and the Psychology of Totalism.* In this type of cliché, "the most far-reaching and complex of human problems are compressed into brief, highly reductive, definitive-sounding phrases, easily memorized and easily expressed."

Like when you say, *Sorry, I'm dating Jesus right now* in order to terminate the possibility of a relationship with all of its messiness, all of its complexity, all of its potential for breaking your heart.

You say, *I'm saving myself for marriage,* as if the heart can only be broken by the act of sex. As if you could ever arrive at the altar completely safe, unscathed by the kind world, unbruised, unbroken.

You tell the Church People you are lonely, and they say, *Let God be your friend* or they say, *What a friend we have in Jesus!* And what you *hear* is that you don't have the right to be lonely, that if your faith was stronger than this, bigger than this, you would be happy.

And it occurs to you that the real work of faith has nothing to do with saying the right words. It has to do with redefining them, chipping away at the calcified outer crust until you find the simple truth at the heart of it all. *Jesus.*

In the delivery room, your baby boy is breathing contented sighs against your chest. For him, the only thing is this simple complex moment: the warmth, the scent of your skin, the light glowing behind his closed eyelids.

He is born. He will spend the rest of his life waking and waking and waking and waking.

Twenty-Two

Prayer Chain: a) A method of communicating prayer
requests quickly and efficiently among Christians; each
person calls one or two other people, and before long
everyone knows what's going on and can (theoretically)
pray accordingly. b) A nineties Christian alternative rock
band known for its angsty music.

We talked every Tuesday when it was lunchtime in the United
States and early evening in London. Kim would call Alissa in her
PR office in Chicago, and Alissa would call me on my cell, and then the
three of us would be connected together like a chain.

When the phone rang that summer Tuesday in Target, I grabbed it
quickly from the diaper bag. My baby, Dane, was corralled in the front of
the shopping cart, waving my shopping list in his small, soft fist.

"Hey, friends!" Alissa chirped.

"Hey!" I slowly walked the aisles, half noticing the things I was tossing into the cart. Wood cleaner. Granola bars. Dish scrubbers wrapped in
crinkly cellophane, which I handed to Dane to play with. Mostly I was
noticing their voices, simultaneously near and far, pressed up against my
ear. "I *miss* you guys. Come see my baby! He's so cute."

"Where are you?" Alissa asked. "Target?"

"Where else?"

"Awww. I want to be at Target with you!" Kim said, and I wished
they were there too. I wanted friendship incarnate, dressing-room friendship, *you-look-adorable-and-you-must-buy-that-top-immediately* friendship.

I wanted them to hold my son and kiss his sticky, fat cheeks. I wanted arm-in-arm wandering and up-all-night talking.

Kim rattled off something. "Whoa," I said. "I got absolutely none of that."

"Sorry." She slowed down, repeated everything deliberately, and I realized the reason I couldn't understand was that her accent had turned almost completely British. "I'm trying really hard to talk American," she said, but she didn't pronounce the *r* in "hard." The altered sound of her speech made me sad. She didn't sound like the girl at the table of the Pizza Pub, slurring swears at the Church People. She'd been living full-time in London for only eighteen months, but the Chicago accent she once had was almost completely gone.

"How's the Man?" Alissa asked.

"Good, good." I wandered around housewares and tried to figure out how to explain my beautiful, unremarkable life. There was nothing particularly exciting to tell them, really. Simple days. Simple nights. Andrew came home from work, and we ate dinner together, all of us pulled up to the kitchen counter, side by side. We took turns putting the baby down for the night, and then we watched television or played backgammon on that old wooden board we bought in China. We didn't keep track of who won or lost, just reset the board and played again.

They were the same routines over and over again, the days strung together like white lights on a string.

The night before, I'd watched quietly from the hallway while Andrew rocked Dane to sleep, his voice soft as he sang "Jesus Loves Me." In the nursery, the lights were dim, and I watched Andrew rest his chin on Dane's small head as he sang, and how do you explain it? The quiet *enough* I felt as I watched?

"Good. And the school?" she added, asking about the master's in fine arts program that I'd been steadily working through.

"Good. Hard. I'm trying to write about our high school days."

"Our high school days," Kim repeated softly, and I could almost hear her reaching back.

"Ha," Alissa said humorlessly. "I found that wineglass that you guys all gave me for my sixteenth birthday. Do you remember? Everyone wrote a little message or prayer or blessing or whatever on a piece of paper, and then you sealed the notes inside the glass with crayon wax. I wasn't supposed to open it until my wedding, but I got sick of having it on my shelf."

"Oh. My. Word," Kim said. She didn't pronounce the *r* in "word." "I'd completely forgotten that we'd done that."

"Me too," I said, thinking about the wineglass, thinking about the naive simplicity of that gift—as if faith was something that could be sealed away like prophecy, kept pure and untouched under a protective seal. As if we could have lived lives so protected that those notes and prayers and blessings would remain true ten years later.

The truth was, everything had been touched. Everything had been changed. But they were still my best friends: Kim. Alissa. They were my deepest community. My church. They were plodding through a world that in so many ways did not make sense. Grappling with it the best they could.

We didn't talk directly about our faith as much anymore, but it was always there. It was the thing we were really discussing when we asked about one another's lives. It was what we meant when we talked about our relationships, when I told them about my son, always changing, always growing. We were believers. We were trying to figure out how to believe.

"Anyway," Alissa said, "the Boyfriend thought the wineglass was really weird."

"Seriously?" I asked.

"I believe the word 'cult' was mentioned."

"He has nooo idea," I said, thinking about vegetable oil on the cafeteria table and Christian ska concerts. Thinking of all of the things we were trying to escape, realizing these same things bound us forever together.

"None whatsoever," said Kim.

"You kind of had to be there," Alissa said, and we were all quiet for a minute.

"We were there," Kim said finally. She sounded sad, nostalgic, and we all felt it deep in our far-flung hearts.

"Yes," I said finally. "We were there."

Twenty-Three

Evangelicalism: One of the largest branches of Christianity in America with more than 70 million adherents.

Y ou are one of them. And also, you are not one of them.

The world is shifting. The kind of evangelicalism that defined your youth is losing ground, falling into shadow. In its place is something new, different. The glass-half-full people call it *new evangelicalism;* the disenchanted cynics call it *postevangelicalism,* as if the whole branch of faith has become irrelevant, as if it is dead, as if you could crack it off of the great oak of your spiritual heritage with one swift tug.

It's like this: The stereotypical evangelical wears Christian T-shirts, has a special Bible cover that says "Jesus Freak" on the front. When he was seven, his Awana Sparks crowns sparkled with fake jewels. He gives you a pamphlet with a cliff on one side and a cliff on the other side. Man. God. In the middle is a great chasm and maybe some hellfire. He asks, "Do you have what it takes to be a missionary wife? to give birth to a baby on the floor of a hut?" He means, "Are you as faithful a Christian as I am?"

The "new evangelical" wears skinny jeans and earrings made from recycled beer caps. After all, she is acquiring a taste for Blue Moon and Chardonnay. She lives in a loft in the city and grows organic vegetables on her balcony because the earth belongs to God, and she wants to take care of it. Her iPod includes songs by crossover Christian band Switchfoot, as well as a couple of albums from Joseph Arthur, quintessential nihilist and unabashed drug addict. She sees truth in them both. She tries to keep things clean, language-wise, but she knows that sometimes, the right word is *fuck*.

You could say the old stereotype is bad. That new evangelicalism is good. But then, this is a simplification also, isn't it? If you have learned anything over the last fifteen years, it's that the world is not made of stereotypes but of *people*, complex and real. And *faith*—that changes too. It has to. It is a cardboard kaleidoscope, ever turning and being turned. You look through it into the Light over and over again, and you never see exactly the same thing.

You are beginning to understand that even the best goals and intentions can be corrupted. That the blind devotion to any Mission can turn dark. You have learned that it is impossible to divide things neatly, and that the second you begin to define something, you limit it. There is no such thing as "cut and dried" in a world of broken humanity. Gray bleeds into gray bleeds into gray, no matter how you slice it.

While American evangelicalism navigates the changing spiritual landscape, your own identity is also in flux. You are neither stereotype. You are edging across the spectrum, drinking wine and paging through the Bible. Not really reading, but also not throwing it across the room. You skim over verses until one strikes you as particularly beautiful or particularly true. Isaiah 57:19, for example: "Peace, peace, to those far and near," says the LORD. "And I will heal them."

You are finished with most of the raging now. There will still be moments when someone says or does something that sparks some hidden anger, and for a few moments, you will rant white-hot over a past spiritual wrong. But then it will flicker and crumble away like ash.

━ ━

You don't exactly choose Grace Community Church. You crash into it.

The two of you have been in your new house for nearly six months before you try a new church. Even then, it is less because you want to and more because you are drawn there. Because no matter how you try to pretend otherwise, these are your people. They will always, somehow, be your people.

But you are tired of the wandering. You've done the church hunt before, and you're afraid of what another drawn-out search will do to you. Though things are better, you're still a little damaged, so you put only two requirements on your church spreadsheet: *Small groups. Close to home.*

The church you find yourself at is a little big and a little fluorescent, and sometimes you feel the need to shield your eyes from the bright light of so many people who are all so *on fire for God.* The electric guitars on stage crescendo into a chorus and a superenthusiastic woman with curly hair announces a new Rick Warren Bible study. The irony of all this is not lost on you: after two years of ranting about *those evangelicals,* you have crash-landed among them.

But also, there is a short, wrinkled man who stands at the front doors every Sunday morning. Even those months when his leg is in a cast and he has to lean on a crutch, he still stands. When you come in, he shakes your hand and he smiles and he looks in your eyes as he says, "Welcome." And you can tell he really means it.

There is a woman who hauls a big trailer into the church parking lot every week, and there are people who bring clothes, food, linens, blankets, towels. People who fill the trailer so the woman can drive it all over the bleeding city, so she can give and give and give. Every night, she stands on the slanted lip of the trailer as the Minnesota winter finds its way through her layers of clothes and burns her skin. She is looking someone in the eye, saying, "Here. This is for you. Because you are loved."

You find yourselves in a small group of young couples, doing all sorts of church-couple things: backyard barbecues and movie nights and Papa Murphy's pizza dinners. You sit in one another's living rooms, and they are just as imperfect and broken as all the Church People you've ever known. But you tell them anyway.

You tell them all about despair, about Depression, about the year of your drinking, about that man you almost kissed. Your husband sits next to you and tells his part of it too, because this is not just your story. It is yours together. You came so close to falling apart; you feel strong and miraculous and sad and *free* sitting there, telling it together.

He's holding your hand, and his grasp is strong. He strokes your thumb when the tears start falling, and you say, "It was really a shit time." And no one flinches when you say the word *shit*. You go on and on, but no one glances absently at the clock and asks if maybe you should move on to question five. No one says, "If you were a fruit, which would you be?" Instead, they look at you attentively; when you are finished, they speak only words of grace.

At Grace Community Church, they are raising money to start a counseling center, so they can help those who cannot afford therapy get to the bottom of their bottomless darkness. So more people can sit on a small couch and look at someone like Rachel Martin while she says, "Let's check in. How was this week?" So they can watch the green lights move back and forth on an EMDR machine and process their pain.

They are building wells so that clean water flows from the dry, cracked earth. They are providing oil changes to single mothers, free of charge. They are looking at the world that is shifting, these people in this church. They are clunking along the best they can, trying their damndest to shift alongside it.

You could leave. There are a million reasons you could come up with to leave. But you decide, for now, to stay.

➤ ➤

You get together with Alissa one hot evening in June. You are back in the Chicago suburbs for a long weekend. Alissa comes in on the train from the city, where she lives in a small loft near the brown line of the el train. She has a cat named Sidney and a handsome, red-headed boyfriend. She gets off the train, smartly dressed, fresh from work. Her heels click on the pavement, and she takes off her sunglasses so you can see the smile stretch deep into her eyes.

"Hey!" she says to you. You squeal and hug each other hard while businessmen with black business briefcases disembark and disperse around you.

You drive a few blocks to the California Pizza Kitchen in downtown Arlington Heights. "I wish Kim were here," you say wistfully. It should be the three of you, sipping wine together on the outdoor patio, the umbrella creating a circle of shadow over you, the sun growing red in the west.

"I know," Alissa says, putting her shades back on. "Poor Kim. She's trapped on an island where they spell 'color' wrong."

You order a bottle of wine and you order appetizers and you talk in the quick back-and-forth of old friends catching up. You talk with your hands, laughing loud over glasses of Pinot Grigio, circling around the details of your lives until you end up, inevitably, at faith.

After all, faith is, will always be, the soil from which your friendship emerged. On some level, you will always be *those* girls, the ones walking together down the halls of Cooper Junior High in your Witness-Wear T-shirts and your Jesus-fish necklaces, your eyebrows arching unplucked over your innocent eyes.

"So, you guys are going to a church?" Alissa asks. She kind of knows the answer. You've mentioned Grace Community offhandedly a couple of times in e-mails and in your regular Tuesday phone conversations.

"Yeah," you say, looking down at your glass. For some reason you're a little hesitant to say it out loud. You're afraid that the camaraderie you found in your mutual hatred for the Church People will disappear if you admit this—that your search has led you back to the place where it all started. A brown church on the side of a road.

"That's cool," she says. She looks at you earnestly over a piece of half-eaten focaccia. "How is it?"

"Oh, you know." You look at her a little sadly as you think about it.

"Hard." You take a slow sip of your wine. "It just felt like we had to either walk away from it totally, or we had to find a way to make it work."

"And you're trying," she says.

"Yeah. We're trying," you say.

"I kind of know what you mean. I feel like it's a little bitchy to be bitter at this point."

You both pause to think about this, wineglasses cradled in your hands. The Jesus-fish necklaces are in the past now. But so are the angry drunken nights, pounding back margaritas at the Pizza Pub. Kim is in London. Alissa is sitting in front of you, sipping her wine, looking so grown-up. The future will be a mix of both of these things: the devotion and the cynicism. You have to find a way for them to coexist within you. Let them destroy each other, and your fragile faith may shatter entirely.

— —

If you read the Bible at all, it's in fits and starts. In many ways, you find yourself still trying to recover from the ways it was hurled at you all those years, the way you hurled it back at others. There was a Way you read the Bible in those high school days. There was a Way you turned the words into cliché, into their own special language, and now a certain amount of baggage remains lodged in the thin pages. You are trying to work through it, but you're not quite there.

But there is also this: the muted browns of the winter fields, covered by patches of snow. Around them, the trees stand bare and graceful in all this cold. You are moving across the frozen landscape in the warmth of your car, in the warmth of your family, your baby boy practicing his consonants quietly behind you. "Dadadada." You look out across the great January cold that usually falls like a shadow over you, and you see *beauty*. And for a flickering moment, you understand God.

Little by little, you will learn to open the Bible, and God will still be there. One day you will open it all the way up again, and it will feel like water washing over you. But for now, you look out at the beauty of the snow-laden fields, stretching as far as you can see. For now, it is enough.

— —

If you search images of Jesus Christ on Google, about 7,190,000 appear in 0.05 seconds. More than you could ever look at, ever begin to comprehend. Da Vinci's Italian Christ with His long brown hair and feminine features. The Ethiopian Jesus from the seventeenth century with His Afro and halo of light. Big, red lips. A yellow-and-red-striped robe. The Chinese Christ presides over the Last Supper, His long black hair parted down the middle. He has a thin Asian mustache, not a bushy beard. His eyes are dark, but kind. The Indian Jesus sits with legs crossed in a meditation pose. His hands are folded, His eyes down. Birds fly near, grazing His still shoulders with the tips of their wings.

You are astounded by the sheer volume of images and perspectives, by the ease with which this God is translated into a hundred thousand cultures. He is big enough, complex enough, wide and broad and deep enough to speak to all of them.

The cover of your Bible now is black leather, and there are no illustrations in which to root your imagination. But there is metaphor. God is covering His people with His feathers in the Psalms, sheltering them under His great, wide wings. In Deuteronomy He is a rock; in the book of John, bread, broken, passed around, given and given and given again. Gate, lamb, light. Physician, prince, rising sun, servant.

Shepherd.

Somewhere in your memory, an image appears. Jesus holding a lamb. He has short black hair and a tidy beard, and even though He's not exactly smiling, you can see the dimple creased into His cheek as He looks down at the lamb in His arms. You believe that one day in the someday world, you will come face to face with God, and you know He will probably look nothing like this picture. But also that there is something to those dimples, to that smile, to that unspoken love on His wind-worn face. He will be smiling at you in a field of light. He will look at you as if He's never loved anything more.

— —

These days, you are aware of the ways you are disappearing into the everyday normal of your average life. The shoveling of snow. The washing of dishes. The earning of money to facilitate the paying of bills.

You catch glimpses of the missionary boys now and again through passed-along fragments or Facebook statuses, and you're not really surprised to see that it's the same for them too. Nick Garcia, for example, is still living in Norway, but his news centers mostly around his one-year-old daughter—the way she likes to stand in front of the glass door of their favorite coffee shop and watch the people pass. Smile, wave. *Hello. Bye-bye.*

When he left all those years ago, you envied his certainty, his ability to look across the rolling sea and see something that you did not: Oslo, Norway. You wished for that kind of precise vision, that kind of calling. You were so afraid it would never come to you. That you would end up in what you called a "plastic, middle-class house in the suburbs," that your life would become cliché.

Now you know life is too complicated to be summed up, written off, no matter where you live. Your son is sleeping in the other room, his arms raised over his head, his fingers closed tightly on his blue knit blanket. There is nothing cliché about him, nothing cliché about *you* as you wake up day after day in the suburbs to the sun rising over the lovely, complex world.

The missionary boys know this just as well as you do. They went out into the world and discovered that life is not so much a mission as beautiful drudgery.

— —

You could chronicle your life in prayer journals. You have forty-three of them stored in that plastic Rubbermaid in the basement. The first one is black leather; it looks almost like a Bible. You started it on Christmas Day, 1997. You were fourteen. On the first page, you thanked God for His eternal love and for your new friend Chris Jacobson.

In the Dominican Republic, you used an eighty-sheet green Mead notebook covered with stickers. When Chris left for Texas, you started a spiral with Raphael's pensive-looking cherub slouched across the cover. You flip to a page and remember the day twenty-three people were at the Buffalo Grove High School Bible study. "How cool would it be," you'd written, "to have to meet in the school theater instead of Mr. Stein's room because there are so many people?" Your cursive is fast and breathless, anxious for revival.

A few months later, you were using a journal given to you by your youth group friend, Megan. It had a great peacock on the front, its feathers fanning like stained glass. "Let your joy for the Lord be as beautiful as these peacock feathers," Megan had written on the first page. This was the journal you were using when Chris broke up with you for the last time.

March of 2000 saw the first of the handmade journals—a piece of fabric from a childhood clown costume laminated for the cover. Then you met Andrew, and all the covers became romantic and mushy: Little kids holding hands. Stills from Audrey Hepburn movies.

When the Depression came, your journal was a notebook with a plain black cover. You'd meant to decorate it but just never could muster up the motivation.

Then there were travel journals, with planes on the covers or with collages of airports and ticket stubs and postmarks. You were not traveling, but you felt as if you were. You felt as if you were on a great journey.

Once, you could get through a prayer journal in two or three months. You had so much to say to God, so much to figure out. You wrote during your classes and at the receptionist desk at Hair Sensations and as you waited for the bus. You rarely included the details of your daily life, but instead lounged in ethereal space between earth and heaven, grasping at vague concepts like *love* and *joy* and *peace*. And *revival*. Especially revival.

Now, things feel different. You don't know what "devotions" look like anymore, but you think it has something to do with telling your story, telling the truth of what happened to you—of who you were, of who you are now. It still has to do with words, with details, with defining and redefining your faith on the page again and again and again and again.

These days, faith is a lot like Wisconsin: a series of repetitive ups and downs, the natural rise and fall of the road that stretches before you. Boring. Beautiful. Ridiculous sometimes, as when the road eases into the Wisconsin Dells and there are suddenly giant plastic animals and water slides and a huge haunted mansion tilted along the road.

And you can't really sum it up in three minutes, can you? None of this fits neatly in the outline titled "My life with Christ" in the Teen Mania Summer Missions Manual. But if you tried, it would look something like this:

    a. Your life BEFORE Christ. You were a child. You climbed the walls of your hallway with bare feet until you were wedged up by the ceiling. You jumped forward from that height, arms out, hoping that maybe you would fly.

    b. HOW you came to know Christ. You had a nightmare. You said a prayer.

    c. Life AFTER you received Christ (changes He has made— what He means to you now). You stood by a flagpole. You ached for revival. You dated a Super-Christian who broke your heart, broke your spirit. You got a little bit stronger, bought some thrift-store sweaters. You met a new man, and he asked you to marry him, and he helped you heal. You went to a church, left a church, went to a church, left a church. Left a church. Left a church. You almost kissed someone else. You went to Memphis and drank yourself sick, and then you came home, and the man you married was there, still there, always there. You took some medicine. And it was dark, dark, dark until the world warmed around you and you began to see it: heaven moving toward earth, holding you together. You went to a church and stayed. You had a baby. You learned to be very still.

Your life AFTER Christ is not static or an end result. You are not suspended in grace above the fray of life. You are looking at God through a kaleidoscope. Your life moves, and the beads shift, and something new emerges. You are defining. Redefining. Figuring it out all over again.

You are in motion, in transit, in flux. You will be sad. You will be happy. You will love and doubt and cry and rage, and all of it matters.

You are human, and you are beloved, and this is what it is to be Alive.

Epilogue

I t is Dane's third summer, and he is barefoot and skinned up and beautiful. His hair is bleached by all the sunlight—by so many mornings spent bent over our backyard pond with his Dollar Store net, catching frogs.

When we walk to our neighborhood park in the after-dinner light, Dane runs ahead of us, all angles and energy. His little brother, Liam, bumbles behind him. He is only one and a half, unsteady still in the walking. After only a minute or two, he sidles up to the red wagon, and Andrew lifts him in.

On the concrete, our shadows stretch long and thin, and we are our own quiet parade. Andrew and I hold hands and he pulls the wagon, and if you look at the shadow, you can see the place where our silhouettes join.

The boys are looking everywhere, taking it in. *Waking.* Around them, the world is wild and new. Full of amazing, beautiful things.

The park we go to is small. It is plastic slides and metal monkey bars and a sun-pocked soccer field with torn nets. It looks like any other playground. It could be anywhere. The boys clamor for the black plastic swings, and we lift them up. Push. *Up, up, up.*

Once, I sat on swings just like these, and I thought they were so small. So ordinary. I thought life was lived out in the great starry beyond. I kicked up toward a Southern Cross I could not see but knew was there somewhere on the other side of my boring, commonplace life.

But now, Andrew is sitting on the swing next to Dane. We have been working, these past few weeks, to teach him to pump. *In. Out. Bend, straighten.* The hard, repetitive work of flying.

He gets frustrated quickly and whines to be pushed, but Andrew keeps encouraging him to try—"In, out, Buddy"—and I know how hard it is. I know what it's like to be weighed down by your own inertia. It is almost inconceivable, sometimes, to believe you are strong enough to propel yourself out.

But sometimes, all it takes is a moment.

You hear the baby's heartbeat for the first time, maybe, and it flutters like wings. And you know it deep in your soul. *I want to get well.*

So you point your toes and kick toward the holy.

And it's not a light switch that you can flick on. It's slow, hard work. It's another Sunday you get up, and you don't want to go to church, but you go anyway. It's another Sunday you stay home in your sweats with your mug of coffee. You open a book that is sort of a little bit about faith because it's the most you can handle right now.

It's one more angry rant over margaritas, and then it's picking yourself up and stumbling forward a few more tentative steps.

And it's then, it's three years later, and the park is humming with the end of summer. Your son kicks forward spastically, and his swing gathers a bit of momentum.

The sun filters through the trees, and every time you look, the pattern of light and leaf is a little bit different. A little bit new.

And you don't even know it's happening until this quiet moment. You feel your heart get still, and instead of the cynical voice in your head, you hear something else entirely. Something old and familiar. And you could almost cry because it's been so long.

But there it is: Unmistakable. Beautiful.

It sounds like *faith* and *hope.*

It sounds most of all, like *Love.*

Author's Note

This is a memoir. To the best of my knowledge and memory, everything written here is true. However, I have changed names and some defining details surrounding the actual people who appear in my story.

I did this first to protect their identities and their privacy. But I also did it to honor the fact that we are all in process. We change and change, and often in the changing, we hurt one another in unintended ways. We say things we didn't mean to say, and we do things we never meant to do. We are broken and healing and always in the process of *becoming*.

It feels complicated to freeze a person—to capture people in a memory and then leave them exposed that way in writing for all time. But these frozen moments are part of what shaped my life and my faith, and I can't tell my story without being honest about them.

I write this knowing that I too have been the Super Christian, bowling over others' feelings with my passion. I have been both the heartbroken and the heartbreaker. I have been unkind and careless more times than I care to admit. I've missed the loneliness of others simply because I wasn't really looking.

In the end, there are no villains or heroes here. Just you. Just me. Just all of us, struggling to make sense of the moments that shape us. May we have the courage to speak true, to forgive one another, and to walk forward in the Love that covers it all.

Discussion Questions

1. In the prologue, Addie describes the See You at the Pole event. She stands at the flagpole, in pouring rain, to pray with fellow Christians for a revival at their high school: "We were fourteen, fifteen, sixteen, standing up for something Great. We were holding hands, holding together God and country, faith and public education, Jesus and his disenfranchised children."

   When no one else shows up, why does Addie stay alone in the rain, trying to pray for her school? What does this act reveal about Addie's faith? Have you had a similar experience? Describe it.

2. How did you feel as you read Addie's description of growing up in an evangelical home? If you were raised in a similar environment, did the traditions—nightly prayers with parents, Sword Drills at Sunday School, flannelgraph Bible stories, the picture of a friendly Jesus—ring true to your experience? How does your story differ from Addie's? What were the good and not-so-good spiritual aspects of your childhood?

   How do you respond to Addie's statement: "It felt so big to you, that fire in your heart. It filled your body, gave you a sort of buoyancy and belonging. A sense of purpose."

3. Have you ever consulted a manual like *The Get-Him Guide*? If so, describe it. Did you feel at age thirteen as Addie did, "so intoxicated by the idea of romance, by the silvery sheen of it, by the way it glimmered like imagined water pooling at the place up ahead where the road dips low, disappears"? What were the guidelines you followed in boy-girl relationships?

    In chapter 3 we meet Chris, Addie's all-American, evangelically advanced boyfriend. What is their relationship based on? What formed the foundation of your personality in junior high and high school? Were you smitten the way Addie was? What was the result?

4. To please Chris, Addie participates in a summer mission. What did you think about the rules of the organization? Were the leaders justified in correcting girls who were "Sunflowers"? Do you think Addie was right to feel guilty after refusing to eat the hard-boiled egg?

    "Only in its most scientific definition does the word *reform* reveal anything of its violent nature. To subject to cracking… An incomplete brokenness. Fracture. Split. Splinter. Snap." When have you been "set straight," only to find yourself figuratively in pieces afterward? What did you learn?

5. Were you surprised when Addie decided to attend an evangelical university? Would you have done the same if you were in her shoes? What were some of the disappointments she faced?

When Addie meets Jared in chapter 11, what happens when she realizes, "It was as if a warning siren had gone off.… All of a sudden it was so clear: I did not want to live in a hut in the jungle. With *anybody*." How has Addie changed from the girl who dated Chris so intently? Do you think she is spiritually stronger or weaker at this point? Why?

6. Addie describes her fellow teachers in China: "This group of college grads moved in the halting, awkward manner of people still… held hostage by the school they came from.… There were rules that made my fussy evangelical upbringing seem wild: No listening to music with drums. No movies with a rating exceeding PG. No public displays of affection." What do you think these rules accomplished? What is your experience with strict rules of conduct? What good do they engender? What not-so-good? How have such rules shaped you as an adult?

7. Addie's and Andrew's stay in China proves spiritually and emotionally suffocating. "The longer we stay here, the more I feel myself disappearing. I need God to reach out of the sky and grab hold of me with one big, invisible hand. It needs to happen

now, before I lose myself in this sadness." What is happening to Addie? Why?

Have you ever felt yourself "going under" in a drastic way? What happened to save you? What happens to save Addie?

8. Why does "the man who is not my husband" appeal to Addie? What is it about the coffeehouse that keeps drawing her in? Have you ever lost track of reality? What caused it? What restored you?

"It is as if Pandora's box has opened, and this world that was so well kept has flown out into the darkness." In this troubled period, what do you think Addie needs the most? Do you feel empathy for her as she struggles, or something else? If you were her friend at this time, what would you have said or done for her?

9. What finally brings a glint of hope to Addie? "Maybe this is the way you move on. You find the small slivers of light, and you hunker down in them.... You wait, knowing that the beams will get wider and wider every day. Knowing that one day, you will wake into the full power of the sun, and you will finally be warm." In what unusual ways or places have you found hope?

10. In chapter 21, Addie concludes being born again "is not Before and After, a clean split, dark and light. It is gradual illumination, fireflies moving slowly toward you, softening the edge of darkness so that you can see the beautiful mystery around you." Does Addie's description resonate with your experience or not? Explain. Do you see mystery as "beautiful" or maddening? Why?

By the end of the book, how has Addie's faith been reshaped? Has yours? Why or why not?

A Conversation
with the Author

Addie, what prompted you to write your story? How are you hoping your story impacts readers?

I began writing the book—kind of on accident—while I was at grad school studying creative nonfiction. I didn't intend to sort out my evangelical past, but the depression came and the bottom fell out, and it all felt tied up together.

So I began to write about all of it, and in the writing, I found structures that allowed me to confess my doubt and anger. I saw connections I hadn't seen before, and I found a way to be honest in a way that I couldn't seem to manage in real life.

And this surprising thing happened: people could relate. Almost no one at my grad school came from a religious background like mine, but everyone had some sort of church baggage. Some well-meant moment gone horribly wrong, some heavy-handed pastor, some overzealous boyfriend.

When I shared bits of my story and others connected with it, it made me feel seen. It made me feel less alone. And that's what I hope that this book does for readers. Memoir, at its best, is never about just one person. It's about all of us—the collective story we're all living.

What was the hardest part of writing it? Did you find it painful? cathartic? freeing?

It was really hard to write about that year of depression and drinking. It's both humbling and terrifying to confront your most broken, destructive self and not look away.

And yet writing this book turned out to be a work of wholeness and healing for me. When I was too angry and cynical to read God's words,

He met me in mine. I didn't see it at the time, but now I recognize this as holy ground.

Are you worried about how the book will be received? How did you make sure you were fair about presenting both the warts-and-all side and the good, helpful side of evangelicalism?

Of course I'm worried—though less because of its criticism of the evangelical culture and more because I've chosen to share my very personal doubts, fears, and failures here. Putting the details of my story out in the world feels weighty and fragile all at once.

But in the end, this book is not a manifesto against evangelicalism; it's not a blueprint for how Christian culture ought to look. It's simply my story. My hope is that by choosing to write vulnerably about my own struggles, I will have given readers a glimpse of a faith that is both broken and beautiful.

Do you regret the years you spent immersed in conservative churches and a Christian college? Why or why not?

No. Well—I sort of wish I'd kept my distance from Teen Mania—but other than that, no.

My feeling is that no matter where you live it, life is a mixed bag. Everything is complex. I learned some of the most beautiful truths in those places. And, with that, I absorbed things that weren't good or pure or true but that seemed like it at the time.

There were people whose words and actions hurt me, but also, there were people who loved me in incredible ways. Often, these extremes existed in the same people...because that's what it is to be human, isn't it? We love each other. We hurt each other. We forgive and learn and move on.

During those years, I fell in love with Jesus, and though it sometimes came out misdirected, it was real and it was sincere and it left its mark on me. In those dark days, it was what kept me from throwing the whole thing away.

And I guess I think it's pointless to regret the past. Wisdom comes from being willing to sort through it: take the good, leave the rest, and move forward.

Many today who grew up in conservative churches are seriously questioning their faith, evidenced by the droves of people in their twenties and thirties leaving the church. What advice would you give to those who are experiencing significant doubts against the faith of their childhood? What would you say to a die-hard member of the evangelical church who might feel wounded by your words?

To the one who is questioning—It feels so lonely, but you are not alone. This is part of becoming whoever it is you're going to become. Give yourself time and space to figure it out. It seems easier, sometimes, to throw the whole thing out altogether, but there is truth and beauty and meaning here for you. The most valuable work you'll do in your life is sorting through the mess to find it.

To the one who loves the evangelical culture—I understand. It was in this place that I fell in love with Jesus for the first time, and if that's where you are, it's a beautiful thing. We are all on our own journeys, and it will look different for all of us. We have to learn to be more gentle with one another.

I met a woman in a coffee shop not too long ago. She had grown up in a nonreligious home and had just started attending an evangelical church. And she loved it. I sat there, humbled, as she talked. That pastoral anecdote that makes me cringe? It made God come alive for her. That verse I'd heard a thousand times—it was new in her ears. The worship, loud and spirited, made her feel as if she were touching God for the first time.

We're all journeying, and none of us have it exactly right. These things that I'm distancing myself from in the evangelical culture are life-giving for others. And someday I might need them again too. Faith is circular like that, and we are, all of us, spiraling round and round toward the hidden heart of God.

At one point in your story, you and Andrew had very different feelings about the home-based church you were attending. Eventually you both withdrew from it. What can spouses do when one feels nourished and the other doesn't?

I think that our individualistic national culture has become pretty engrained in the North American experience and practices of Christianity—particularly the evangelical flavor of it. The focus on personal quiet time, individual study, and this idea of "my faith" or "my personal relationship with God" have, in many ways, isolated us from working through questions together—even in our closest relationships.

I don't think there's a perfect answer to this. I don't have a prescription, only our own experience. For us, change came slowly and required sacrifice. It meant Andrew leaving a church that he loved because I couldn't find a way to connect there. It meant taking some time away and finding a common ground where we could step forward (tentatively) again—together.

I think that Andrew and I both used to think that the first most important thing was to love God, and the second most important thing was to love others. But during those hard months, we learned that it was all bound up together. That figuring out how to love each other in the change and in the struggle gave us a new understanding and grasp on God's grace and faithfulness.

Near the end of the book, you conclude, "Your life AFTER Christ is not static, or an end result.... You are in motion, in transit, in flux. You will be sad. You will be happy. You will love and doubt and cry and rage, and all of it matters. You are human, and you are beloved, and this is what it is to be Alive." How has discovering the flexibility of faith freed you from a boxed-up faith? Why is that healthy?

When Jesus is presented to you in your early days as "The Answer" and "The Cure," it's shocking and debilitating when you find yourself—later on—struggling with questions and empty places.

It's not necessarily that the old metaphors are bad, it's just that they aren't enough. There are so many sides to all of this, so many layers. Discovering that God was bigger and more mysterious than my little box of prepackaged answers, catch phrases, testimonies, and apologetics was the hardest thing that has ever happened to me. And also the best.

What is the value of tracing one's spiritual lifeline, noting where your faith was challenged or changed?

It always bothered me, the way the evangelical three-minute testimony hinged on one moment: the one in which you "accepted Christ." For me that moment happened when I was five years old, and I barely remember it, and it felt strange and awkward to make it the climax of a story that I was telling to strangers.

I don't doubt it was important—that moment, that day. My child heart was reaching for something that it did not understand but believed to be true. A safe place, a good place. A home. It is the blurry beginning of something beautiful, and I keep this memory fragment close to my heart.

And yet, it was only one moment, and faith is not just one day in which your life was changed. It is that magnetic, changing pull of love every moment of every day. So it seems right, to me, to trace the thin thread of faith that unravels through your years. It seems important to notice every moment you can—the beautiful ones, the hard ones, the quiet ones—because these matter too.

The older I get, the less it seems to matter how I found God. What matters most is the ways He is always finding me.

Where are you now in your spiritual life? What kind of church do you attend? What qualities attracted you to it?

I would say that I'm still in the place of rebuilding and redefining what I believe. Writing, in particular, has been instrumental in this process. Through my blog, I've been working through some of the old clichés, metaphors, and Christian language. It has given me a way to sort through this more thoughtfully, to interact with a broader community, and to see God in new ways.

Our church journey was a long, difficult one. The church we ended up at in the final chapters of this book is not the one we attend now—though it was a safe place to land for a while. We connected with a few other couples and had a chance, for the first time, to share our story vocally and honestly. Our years there played a major role in my own journey of relearning to love "Church People" and in my making peace with certain aspects of the evangelical world.

The church we're at now is a small community church, and it's really not all that different than any other church. But when we walked in, I could feel my heart expanding—and it was almost inexplicable to me, the suddenness of it. The pastor spoke, and he wasn't saying anything new, but for the first time in years, I could hear it.

And I think in the end, you're not really looking for "the right church." You're looking for yourself. Finding a church is about finding a place where your specific, beautiful heart can hear good news and take it all the way in. A place where they talk about God in a language you understand. A place where you can serve with your whole, broken heart and be healed in all that giving.

I don't really know. All I know is that we landed in this tiny church one Sunday morning and I felt entirely myself. And we've been there ever since.

If you could talk to Chris today, what would you say?

Poor Chris. He comes off as such a jerk in this book. But really, he was just a boy. His passion for God got all mixed up with the intensity of that first love, and it made him feel larger than life to me. It amplified his impact on my life in ways that he certainly never intended or imagined.

If I could talk to him, I'd tell him that it matters—what happened with us—but that I know that he didn't mean for it to go the way that it did. I know he loved God; I believe he genuinely loved me in that confusing teenage way we all loved one another then. He was just figuring it out the best he could at age seventeen, eighteen, nineteen. We all were.

I'd thank him for handing me that cardboard kaleidoscope of faith when I was so young and for showing me the beauty of it all. I'd tell him I forgive him. I'd tell him to never ever again point out blackheads on a girl's nose. And then I'd smile, wave, and walk away.

—◆—

For more information about Addie Zierman and public readings of *When We Were on Fire,* or to schedule a reading in your city, please visit AddieZierman.com.

Acknowledgments

S o many people have waded with me through the exhausting, exciting, wonderful, intense process of creating this book. I'd like to thank them here.

To my fabulous agent, Rachelle Gardner—thank you for taking a chance on me. To the wonderful people at Convergent, particularly my editor, Dave Kopp—thank you for loving and believing in this book.

To my readers at AddieZierman.com—the agent said "build a platform," and I cried for a week because I didn't think I could do it. How could I know that you would be among the best things to ever happen to me? Thank you for your comments, your kindness, your support, your excitement. Thank you for reading my words online and now, finally, here.

To Judy Hougen—thank you for introducing me to the magical world of *creative nonfiction* and for creating a safe space to work through my own journey. To the wonderful teachers at the Hamline University MFA program (specifically Barrie Borrich)—thank you for steering this project to a first, full manuscript.

To my writing group friends, Beth, Jo, and Andy—thank you for reading *all the drafts* and listening to *all the angst*. To Carra—thank you for helping me navigate the publishing world as well as my own heart. To Anna—thanks for being an unfailing source of encouragement for me in this process.

To my Mama Friend, Kenna—all those years ago you said, "Let me take your kid all day!" And when I tried to decline, you said, "This is happening. Don't look a gift horse in the mouth." Without your support and friendship, this book would not exist. Thanks for being My Person.

To Kim and Alissa—thanks for coming with me that time I wanted to put vegetable oil on the cafeteria table. Thanks for M&M'S out the van window and for Metropolis, Illinois. Thank you for margaritas and the Dells and for being there the whole time—even when we were apart.

To the Zierman family, for embracing me as one of your own—thank you. And to my own parents—though you're not in the pages of this book much, your love is at the heart of my identity. Much of my faith journey has changed, but the solid boards that hold the whole thing up are there because you put them there. Thank you.

To my sister, Paige—your wisdom and kindness inspire me. To my brother, Erik—your love for others astonishes me. I love you both farther than all the miles.

To my sons, Dane and Liam—you give me courage. Wherever you journey leads, may you always ache for your true home—the Love of God. (Thanks for being good for the baby-sitter.)

To my husband, Andrew (who might not have married a writer if he'd known all this was coming)—thank you for writing retreats and early mornings and baby-sitters. Thank you for believing in this for me when I couldn't believe it for myself. Thank you for letting me share the details of our story so that others might feel less alone in theirs. Every day, you choose this faith and love over again, and I am desperately grateful.